RIPE FR
HARVEST

0-8054-1656-0

Published by Broadman & Holman Publishers, Nashville, Tennessee

Dewey Decimal Classification: 269
Subject Heading: CHURCH GROWTH

Unless otherwise noted, Scripture quotations are from the New
American Standard Bible, © the Lockman Foundation, 1960, 1962,
1963, 1968, 1971, 1972, 1973, 1975, 1977; used by permission.
Citations from other versions are identified by the following
acronyms: NEB, the New English Bible, © The Delegates of the
Oxford University Press and the Syndics of the Cambridge University
Press, 1961, 1970, reprinted by permission; NIV, The Holy Bible,
New International Version, © 1973, 1978, 1984; NKJV, New King
James Version, © 1979, 1980, 1982, Thomas Nelson, Inc.,
Publishers; and RSV, Revised Standard Version of the Bible, copy-
righted 1946, 1952, © 1971, 1973.

Library of Congress Cataloging-in-Publication Data
Drummond, Lewis A.
    Ripe for harvest : the role of spiritual awakening in
church growth / Lewis A. Drummond.
        p. cm.
Includes bibliographical references.
ISBN 0-8054-1656-0 (pbk.)
1. Church growth. 2. Church renewal. I. Title.
BV652.25 .D78 2001
269—dc21

00–058542

1 2 3 4 5 6 7 8 9 10 05 04 03 02 01

RIPE FR HARVEST

THE ROLE OF SPIRITUAL AWAKENING IN CHURCH GROWTH

LEWIS A. DRUMMOND

BROADMAN
&HOLMAN
PUBLISHERS

NASHVILLE, TENNESSEE

This book is dedicated to my students.
They have been a source of rich inspiration and encouragement to me through many years. May our Lord use them mightily in kingdom service wherever the Holy Spirit may lead them.

"Open your eyes and look at the fields!
They are ripe for harvest."
JOHN 4:35 NIV

CONTENTS

FOREWORD

In the book *Ripe for Harvest* the author, Lewis Drummond, has put two great principles together and given us an unusual contribution that will help every leader understand the spiritual nature of church growth. Drummond has combined the spiritual nature of revival with the analytical nature of church growth to help everyone see how God grows a church.

There have been scores of books written on revival, where many authors describe revival as something mysterious and elusive. Revival is something most church leaders want and pray to get for their church, but they do not know practically how to get it, nor do they know how to direct revival to grow a church when it comes. But Drummond correctly defines *revival* as "God pouring Himself out on His people." "I will pour out My Spirit on all flesh" (Acts 2:17 NKJV). "Times of refreshing may come from the presence of the Lord" (Acts 3:19 NKJV).

Drummond shows the reader that revival is good . . . healthy . . . and will grow a church. His warm knowledge of revival comes from the many revival crusades he has preached in America and abroad. But Drummond also knows revival from his intimate acquaintance with the historical volumes that tell the glories of revivals past. *Ripe for Harvest* will warm the heart of church leaders and make them yearn for the revivals they experienced previously or for the revival they have never tasted.

Many books have been written on church growth, so that many authors tie the growth of a church to the laws or principles of evangelism and expansion. They make church growth sound like the pages of a business manual of a corporation or the directions given to a corporate vice president. Yes, church growth involves the discipline of finding the principles of church planting, growth, outreach, and the understanding of its decline. But Drummond has made the principles of church growth sing. Like Handel's *Messiah* where there is a perfect mixture of the science of music with the touch of the divine—a blend of head and heart—Drummond has blended revival with church growth to demonstrate how divine fingers sculpt the church, while at the same time the church follows the guidance of his laws for growth.

When the world looks at the church, they primarily want to see God at work. They do not want to see the church's budget, programs, or organizational chart. If the world wanted to see "business as usual," they would look to the corporations around them. When the world enters the church, they ought to feel God . . . to experience worship . . . to touch the divine. Lewis Drummond has pointed us in the right direction and told us it can happen. However, he cannot guarantee revival for our churches, nor will he guarantee growth will happen. Revival is personal—like breathing—we must reach out to touch God, then let God touch us. When God comes to us, we can have revival and church growth.

Not all revivals can be felt. Sometimes it comes internally and only a few individuals are revived. Then we can see revival in their lives and rejoice with them for what God has done in their lives. But there are other times when *atmospheric revival* visits the church. Then you can feel it like the morning mist as it refreshes your face and life. Drummond shows how revival and church growth go hand in hand both to renew the church and to cause it to grow.

I pray that God will use this book to its intended purpose. May its readers become revived and, in turn, may they awaken the church. Then may an awakened church grow to its fulfillment.

ELMER L. TOWNS
Dean, School of Religion
Liberty University,
Lynchburg, Virginia

PREFACE

What makes a church "ripe for the harvest"? How does a congregation reach out and reap results? Compelling questions; important questions! An effective pastor in England, a man who has seen every church he served grow significantly—which is a very unusual phenomenon in Europe today—answered the query with these words: "Nothing impacts society so profoundly as a sustained period of *true spiritual revival*. The leadership of the church plays a vital role in such movements of the Holy Spirit. True spiritual revival comes only from God, but the church has a *key part to play* in recognizing and encouraging the principles God uses to stimulate and sustain spiritual and numerical growth. The church 'was strengthened; and encouraged by the Holy Spirit, it grew in numbers, living in the fear of the Lord' (Acts 9:31 NIV). To unleash this powerful potential of the local church, we must translate fine ideals into everyday practical reality."[1]

The Britisher had it right—for England, America, or any place in the world. The field is made ripe for reaping by a true moving of God in awakening power. But the Holy Spirit does not do his reviving work in a vacuum; he uses his people to implement the movement. This means that God's powerful acts, coupled with the church's intelligent actions, form the warp and woof of a real reaping of revival harvest. That dynamic combination weaves a tapestry of beautiful church growth.

The goal of this book is to bring together the spiritual elements of revival and good church growth methodologies. This is something of a different approach today. The rationale for this statement rests in the fact that a host of books have been written on both subjects, but they rarely seem to interact. Yet a church has its greatest explosive growth in the context of a spiritual awakening. This work intends to fuse the two principles of spiritual awakening and church growth methods in such a fashion as to demonstrate that the church field of any congregation can be made "ripe for harvest" when a congregation shapes its approach to ministry on these two central principles. This fusion of truths is the rationale for this entire work. If this approach can be successfully accomplished, the effort to produce the book will certainly not be in vain. Hopefully, God will be glorified in the significant extension of his kingdom.

Appreciation must be expressed to my two secretaries who have been so helpful and faithful in laboring over the manuscript. My deep gratitude goes to Mrs. Michelle Joiner and Mrs. Sherrell Hallquist; without them, I could never have completed the task.

May God bless the efforts of your church as you launch out on these principles. May your church grow and flourish from a kingdom perspective, thus fulfilling its role. This book goes forth with that prayer.

LEWIS A. DRUMMOND
Billy Graham Chair of Evangelism
Beeson Divinity School, Samford University
Birmingham, Alabama

CHAPTER 1

WHEN CHURCHES ENJOY EXPLOSIVE GROWTH

The place: Paducah, Kentucky. The year: 1905. The venue: First Baptist Church. At that place, time, and situation the venerable old pastor of the First Baptist Church, Dr. J. J. Cheek, got caught up in something startlingly unusual.

It had all begun one year earlier in Wales, the western projection of the main isle of the British Isles. Unusual things were erupting over the land that had people aghast. A young ministerial student, Evan Roberts, had encountered God in a fresh way. Radically transformed in his spiritual experience, Roberts began to preach and minister with the touch of heaven upon him. Thousands flowed into the kingdom of Christ through the ministry of that young preacher as a new movement of God spread over the land. The divine moment had come. We know the phenomenon today as the historic Welsh Revival of 1904.

Within a year, the spirit of the awakening had crossed the Atlantic and was coursing through the American countryside. Deeply touched by God's reviving grace, Dr. Cheek cried out in Kentucky, "I will give myself to the salvation of souls." But could one really expect much? After all, Dr. Cheek was an old man and perhaps somewhat naïve. Moreover, Paducah, Kentucky, in 1905 could not boast of being a large town; nor was the First Baptist Church a megachurch in the sense of today's standards. But Dr. Cheek meant what he said. He threw himself into the task. The result? In the next two months, this man of God received into the fellowship of the First Baptist Church of Paducah about one thousand new members. The city stood startled. They had never seen anything on this scale, even though one hundred years earlier America's Second Great Awakening had much of its beginnings in Kentucky.

Dr. Cheek served so ardently and fervently that he actually succumbed to his labors and died. *The Western Recorder,* the Kentucky Baptist paper, eulogized him with these words: "A glorious ending to a faithful ministry." He left a legacy that remains to this day. But what happened? What was behind this incredible influx of new church members? How did so many people come to discover true faith in Jesus Christ? What is the key to such phenomenal *church growth?*

THE QUEST FOR CHURCH GROWTH

The growth of the church has been a keen interest and a goal of believers since the first century. Although this concern has taken on many dimensions and approaches since the early days of the church, it does present a worthy endeavor. In the light of that fact, it is wise to turn to the New Testament, since God's Word alone forms the only sure foundation in the search for church growth in all ages and cultures. On the day of Pentecost, for example, Luke records that three thousand people were enrolled in the kingdom of God and the church on that one particular day. Moreover, the Lord "was adding to their number day by day those who were being saved" (Acts 2:47). Although one must be alert and not get caught up in the "numbers game," a genuine quest for church growth has biblical validity. The rationale is simple: Proper church growth means the lost world being reached for Christ and thus accomplishing the ultimate goal— kingdom growth. The enhancement and spread of God's rule constitutes the final purpose of *all* endeavors at growth. But beware; it must be *proper kingdom* growth.

Recent years have brought a new emphasis on the growth of the church. Volumes on this subject line the shelves of bookstores.

Although concern for kingdom progress has to some extent always characterized God's people, it seems today that the kingdom aspect of growth has been minimized. All the emphasis appears to revolve around *local* church growth. But the modern church growth movement did not start out that way; kingdom consciousness rested at its heart. The movement boasts an interesting history.

THE BACKGROUNDS

The modern church growth movement, although most think of it as an American phenomenon, actually had its beginning in India. This may seem an unlikely place for such a strong movement to be launched, but in the 1930s an American missionary to India, Dr. Donald McGavran, birthed the movement. McGavran, who was in his middle thirties, observed that some churches on his field grew while others did not. Of course, there is nothing unusual about this phenomenon; it occurs worldwide. But McGavran began to ask serious questions about why some churches grew and others seemingly did not. He believed the progress of the kingdom revolved around the issue. So he set out to find an answer to his questions.

After considerable and lengthy research, he penned his findings in a book entitled *The Bridges of God*.[1] This watershed volume kicked off the current movement. Although McGavran's work was primarily a mission-oriented emphasis, the principles he espoused soon spread. As the word got around, McGavran came to the United States and received a challenge to create the Institute of Church Growth in Eugene, Oregon. He responded and launched the program. Up until 1972, the primary emphasis of the church growth movement was on missionary activity. But it became clear that McGavran's concepts were applicable to churches everywhere. He was invited to the Fuller Theological Seminary, where he settled and became the father of the modern church growth movement.

It should be clearly understood that McGavran's primary concern centered in *evangelistic* church growth. But he faced a problem. The term *evangelism* carried so much baggage in his day, meaning so many different things to different people, that he struggled to come up with a new nomenclature that would express his views on how people can be reached for Christ and thus grow the kingdom. To solve the problem he coined the phrase "church growth." For McGavran, church growth meant evangelism. And it caught on. Before long he was writing, teaching, preaching, and holding conferences all over the United States. In that context he penned his *magnus opus, Understanding Church Growth.*[2] Students flocked to sit under McGavran's teaching. Fuller Seminary had broken new ground in theological education. Most seminaries and Bible schools today include church growth courses in their curriculum, and the average pastor has read many books on the subject.

CONTEMPORARY ISSUES

All of this fits in quite well with the social dynamics that have permeated many aspects of Western life generally, and American society in particular. For example, in the West, we tend to place high value on success. Everyone desires to succeed; no one wants to be a failure. And, of course, this is not all bad. Yet "success" and "failure" can easily be misunderstood, especially as it relates to the life of the church. Everybody wants his or her church to grow—and rightly so. But at times we have equated success with numerical growth alone. We love to see our statistics on the up side. Growth has become so important to the life of many churches today that it appears to have become the number-one priority.

Of course, churches should reach people for Christ and thereby grow. After all, the Great Commission commands it (Matt. 28:19–20; Acts 1:8). God's Spirit operates in and through the life of the local church to bring the lost sheep home. Heaven rejoices when one single person experiences salvation in Christ (Luke 15:7). Our Lord smiles on such growth. We must never lose the vision. But a danger lurks in the shadows. We can put such emphasis on numerical growth that we forget the kingdom aspect of the enterprise. It can even degenerate into the psychology that unless a church experiences great numerical growth, someone has failed and he or she must pay the price for this "failure."

Thus, a general negativism can arise when a church reaches a plateau or slips into decline. This often brings on a serious spirit of unrest in the congregation. In almost any geographical area, one can find churches that are growing. So the questions of the declining church becomes: Why are *we* not growing? What's wrong? What are we doing wrong? How can we see our field once again ripe for the harvest? This questioning unrest can escalate, leading to a serious issue in the church that may manifest itself in a number of ways.

THE NEGATIVE FALLOUT

As the unrest grows in the non-growth church, it often results in a fleeing of the membership, thus deepening the problem. It becomes easy to criticize such people for abandoning the sinking ship when loyalty would require one to go down with it. But not every church member has this kind of commitment to his or her church. The Boomer generation does not have the same institutional loyalty as older age groups. So they begin to look to other congregations that are on the upswing, and they affiliate there. The success syndrome has triumphed again.

A second negative aspect relates to the leadership. Many people love to place blame on the church's leaders. If a church fails to grow, some members conclude it must be the fault of the pastor and/or the staff. This negative spirit implies that no one wants to take responsibility; therefore, let's find a scapegoat. So the pastor and staff members become the culprits. It can develop into far more than just placing blame; it can lead to termination. In the particular denomination of this author, some two thousand pastors and staff each year are either terminated or forced to resign. And in numerous cases, the reason revolves around an unhappy membership that complains there has been no growth. That is a deplorable situation, and it indicates a shallow concept of what constitutes genuine church growth as well as ignorance of the nature of the kingdom of God.

The general situation often reduces itself to the fact that the church turns in on itself, and in "naval-gazing" fashion, visualizes itself as failing. More than one church has finally self-destructed. Even if a local congregation does not degenerate to this extreme, it may begin to try everything imaginable to generate growth. Compromises and cutting corners to reach people become the pattern. Numerical growth is sought at almost any cost. But it appears that the majority of declining churches simply resign themselves to their supposed fate and give up—not without an abundance of self-justifying excuses. All this certainly does not lead to spiritual health in the church.

WHAT ABOUT THE KINGDOM?

The ultimate tragedy of this negativism or superficial quest for growth centers in the fact that the kingdom of God suffers. Further, when an *inordinate* quest for growth grips a congregation, it can bring about a kind of growth that falls short of the New Testament standard for genuine kingdom growth. Churches need to understand that true kingdom growth matters more than institutional growth. Although the two cannot be completely separated, kingdom growth should be the ultimate goal. When a church reverses the order, lowers its standards, and puts the local church and its growth above the high standards of entrance into the kingdom of God, both ultimately suffer harm. True church growth from the biblical perspective means kingdom growth as people are genuinely evangelized on a firm, mature, biblical basis. Then they join the local church because they have entered the kingdom of God itself. The result is that both the visible church *and* the kingdom go forward for God's glory.

ANOTHER ASPECT

Church growth that comes about by believers joining a local congregation from another church should never be discouraged or denigrated, even though this may not mean kingdom growth *per se*. This phenomenon can be significant for the life of the church and surely for the people joining. Of course, this assumes the move comes about from pure motives and through the leadership of the Holy Spirit. Yet, churches should recognize this is not kingdom growth as such. This type of growth has been facetiously described as "swapping sheep from one pasture to another." Nonetheless, it certainly has its place and can be meaningful. But a church should not rely on this kind of growth alone; it could lull a congregation into laxity about reaching the unconverted for Christ.

What can be done about this inordinate quest for purely institutional "success"? Something obviously needs to be done. Mature church growth leaders have a proper balance on this issue and warn us against the hidden pitfalls. Pastor Rick Warren of the Saddleback Community Church in Orange County, California, serves as a classic example. God has used his leadership to create a truly great megachurch. In his book *The Purpose Driven Church* he outlines his approach. It has become a definitive work in the field.[3] Shortly in this chapter we will analyze Warren's basic principle. But this raises the immediate question about the so-called megachurch and its validity in the growth phenomenon.

THE MEGACHURCH

Today the quest for growth has precipitated the much-heralded megachurch. Most people see the megachurch movement as an American phenomenon of the last half of the twentieth century. Such is not the case, however. Historically, there have always been megachurches. A cursory survey of kingdom extension through two millennia makes this evident. But the current emphasis on the super-church had something of its beginning in the ministry of Charles Haddon Spurgeon of Victorian England.

Spurgeon arrived in London as a nineteen-year-old fledgling preacher. He had received an invitation to become the pastor of the New Park Street Baptist Church in London's Southside. The congregation had an illustrious history. Great preachers such as John Gill, Benjamin Keach, John Rippon, and others had served as ministers of the thriving congregation. But when Spurgeon came on the scene, the church had fallen upon hard times; decline and decay had set in. Although the church building seated fifteen hundred people, when Spurgeon preached his first sermon, only eighty people heard his message. Yet within a year, two thousand people were crowding into that church building. On many Sundays hundreds were turned away for lack of seating space.

After a few short years in the old venue, the great Metropolitan Tabernacle was built. It seated six thousand people, and Spurgeon saw it filled every Sunday morning and Sunday evening through the next thirty years of his London ministry. It became something of a paradigm for the megachurch of today. Moreover, Spurgeon's ministry proved to be one of profundity and depth. People did not lightly join the Metropolitan Tabernacle congregation. A high standard, one that brought about genuine kingdom growth, was lifted up. The church practiced an evangelism of biblical integrity. It stands as a monument to New Testament evangelism. Spurgeon personified and ably implemented that spirit, and the church grew rapidly. In its heyday it grew into the largest evangelical church in the world.

Today, virtually every city of reasonable size in America has at least one or more megachurches. The same can be said for certain places in Europe and for many of the emerging nations. As the epicenter of the Christian movement seems to be shifting to the Pacific Rim and to the Southern Hemisphere, incredible megachurches are being birthed and grown in those parts of the world. South Korea boasts the largest single congregation in the history of Christianity. With approximately one million members, Pastor David Yungi-Cho preaches to his congregation of multiplied thousands every week. The megachurch phenomenon, when built on a firm biblical basis, can be mightily used of God. It cannot be legitimately criticized simply because the congregation is large. Such churches often reach many for Christ, and genuine kingdom growth occurs.

But for growth to have lasting kingdom results, it must be built on *scriptural* foundations. A genuine striving for biblical *integrity* must characterize church membership. The Holy Spirit intends the congregation to place Christ at the head of the church in the full New Testament sense. Of course, not every church will become a megachurch. Some churches will grow little in numbers because sociological and geographical factors preclude great numerical growth. But all churches can reach some people for Christ, and all can see *spiritual* and *ministry* growth—the kind of kingdom growth that God honors.

But reaching people for Christ and his salvation seems increasingly difficult today. What is the problem?

A CONTEMPORARY PROBLEM

In the contemporary quest for evangelistic church growth and effective ways of reaching people, everyone realizes the task is not as easy as it once was. Why? First of all, cultural generation gaps have developed into a real issue. Contemporary religious sociologists divide the different generations of society into the following categories:

- The Builder generation: Those born before 1946.
- The Boomer generation: Those born between 1946 and 1964.
- The Buster generation: Those born after 1964.
- The Bridger generation: Those now in their teens or early twenties.[4]

Some legitimacy can be found in categorizing society into generational segments in this fashion. Considerable differences exist in the basic mentality of these various groups, at least in a broad sense. The Builders do not understand the Boomers. The Boomers surely do not want to be like the Builders; their whole approach to life appears different. Moreover, the sociologists tell us that the Busters do not like the Boomers; they view the Boomers as too materialistic. It remains to be seen what the basic attitude of the Bridgers, the postmoderns, will ultimately be.

These generation gaps precipitate a difficult situation in communication and especially in worship. Churches today face something of the same communicative challenge that missionaries face when they enter a new nation with a different culture and language. How do we "culturalize" the message so it communicates effectively? Further, the problem is heightened by the fact that the average church in the average town has all four of these generations under one roof. Can these four groups be adequately ministered to, and can they be enlisted to participate in true church growth? This problem surfaces most clearly in the so-called revolution in worship.

THE WORSHIP ISSUE

Most churches find themselves in a serious state of transition concerning the basic format of their worship experiences. It has often precipitated serious problems. As a case in point, the Builders love the grand old traditional hymns and they love to sing out of the hymnbook. The Boomers want to sing praise choruses with the lyrics projected on a screen. They love to stand during the singing of the choruses. It has been facetiously said that you can stand so long that the poor Builder generation almost collapses in the pew from exhaustion. Busters must have a guitar and a keyboard to accompany them in their singing. What the Bridgers will eventually want remains a question—hard-rock gospel music seems to best fit their taste at the moment. So the revolution in worship goes on.

Some churches, sensitive to the issues, have given themselves over to so-called "seeker services," usually appealing to the Boomer and Buster generations. Hymnbooks are out; choruses are in; and standing, not sitting, during the worship time has become the vogue. No choir but a small group of worship leaders are the mode. Preaching gets minimized at times. Moreover, drama and various new communicative approaches set the style. And it often means that the older generation, and even some of the younger generation, reject it.

Among some of the young Busters and Bridgers, a turn to a more liturgical form of worship can be found. This turn of events has resulted in an influx into the Greek Orthodox church, where the liturgy is staid and traditional. Other churches attempt to blend the various approaches, with the result that no one seems happy. All these attempts are admirable in motive. But we must find ways to reach all people of diverse backgrounds because all people of every generation need Christ. We devote an entire chapter to the worship issue later in this book.

Of course, it can be argued that churches ought to target the generation they wish to reach. Neighbor and Thomas call such an approach, "the most thrilling concept of evangelism known to man: target-group evangelism."[5] In some senses, this quote may be true. But this method of outreach demands a large group of the generation targeted. And this, in turn, demands a large population from which to draw—such as in the bigger cities. What about the average church in an average town? Many churches do not have the luxury of being located in a large populous area, nor do they have the resources to focus upon just one group. Tens of thousands of congregations face this reality.

Regardless of the sociological, communicative issues, the gospel must be clearly communicated with relevance and in its purity and entirety. Let this basic truth be strongly emphasized before we seek answers to our contemporary problems. Moreover, the Word of God must be expressed so that people of different cultures and backgrounds will understand and grasp the message. But again, it must be the gospel: the truth of the life, death, and resurrection of Jesus Christ coupled with a genuine call to repentance and trusting faith in Christ. There must never be a compromise on the essence of the Good News, even though it must be expressed in a context that is understandable to that given culture. This alone assures growth with integrity.

A CAUTION

At this very point, a subtle but serious mistake in the presentation of the message of Christ can be made. As an example, in our appeal to the Boomer and Buster generations, Christ is often presented merely as One who can help people in their difficulties so they can "feel good." Of course Christ can help a person with any problem. He came to give life and to give it "abundantly" (John 10:10). But an overemphasis on that psychological theme can cause us to compromise the deeper problem of sin, the judgment of God upon sin, and eternal punishment for sin in the place that the Bible calls hell. God is love, but he is also righteous and just. The Scriptures present God as a benevolent, loving Father, but also as the Holy One. The Lord Jesus Christ was fully man and can empathize with every aspect of human life, but he was also the sinless Son of God who for the brief period of his thirty-three years on Earth laid aside his full heavenly glory to atone for our sins.

All of these truths must never be minimized. The balance of the entire biblical revelation must be kept before people. Moreover, we exist as God's creations—mere creatures—and we owe him glory and honor whether we "feel good" or not. The Christian experience is far more than having good feelings. We must never lower biblical standards in order to appeal to certain aspects of people's personality traits, although the Bible declares that the gospel of Christ certainly appeals to whatever the human need may be. He does bring true, lasting peace to a person's life (John 14:27). Still, the most basic human need centers in the forgiveness of sin. Making all these realities paramount may not bring about as much "growth" as one would hope. Still, in a balanced fashion, the full biblical truth must be lifted up as the standard.

All of these problems often grow out of a secularized orientation in evaluating church life. This, in turn, precipitates shallow, superficial methodologies and a misunderstanding of the kingdom goal of the church. Numbers are important, but they are not everything. Church growth is important and vital, but as stressed, growth must be seen as *kingdom growth*, and this means people being brought to genuine faith in Jesus Christ. Simply put, the quest for growth must travel along proper avenues, and those avenues are basically biblical.

Where can we find some answers to all these serious, fundamental problems that the church faces today in its quest for growth? The rest of this book attempts to provide some answers to the issues. There are roadblocks to be faced and overcome before growth will occur. Certain realities must be addressed.

REALITIES OF OUR QUEST FOR GROWTH

To begin with, only a small percentage of churches in the West are actually growing. For example, the virtual demise of congregations in Western Europe is most disturbing. The great Spurgeon Tabernacle has only some two or three hundred people worshiping on any given Sunday—and this just one hundred years after the death of Spurgeon. Britain desperately needs change. As Jack Burton, a British minister, said concerning the need of his country today, "A renewal of interest in religion and a rediscovery of its potency . . . would set human life in its true . . . context and provide glimpses of God, and a vibrant living faith."[6]

Many congregations throughout Europe face the same situation. They have a mere handful of worshipers in their churches and can barely keep the doors open. Notable exceptions exist, for which we thank God. Nonetheless, the church in Western Europe stands in serious peril.

In the United States, which we often visualize as the citadel of Christianity, only a small percentage of churches show significant growth today. Most congregations have either reached a plateau or are in decline. The average church is a long way from being a megachurch. The typical American church has only about one hundred regular attendees. And though we still may think of North America as a Christian arena, the battle does not seem to be going too well at the moment for many congregations. Not many churches experience growth; even many mainline denominations have slipped into decline. A recent survey revealed that in an eighteen-month period, eight million members have left their churches in the United States. Furthermore, a church may at times begin to grow, only to see that growth fizzle out. One pastor will come and the church will experience growth; the next pastor comes and the back door appears busier than the front.

Of course, lack of numerical growth does not necessarily spell no spiritual growth. To Donald McGavran's credit, when he gave birth to the modern church growth movement, though he centered on numerical growth, spiritual growth concerned him as well. Ministry growth also constituted part of his agenda. He wanted to see the ministry of the church reaching out to touch needy lives. He desired to generate genuine discipleship as the church moved forward in its total growth experience. And this must always be the quest. But how often does it happen?

As a case in point, the so-called "average" church today, if it is fortunate, has about half of its members in attendance at Sunday morning worship service. If the church has an evening worship time, that number is cut at least in half again. Ninety percent of the contributions of the average church come from ten percent of the congregation, and the same percentages hold for any kind of dynamic service in and through the life of the local church. This is a far cry from the biblical principle of discipleship that Jesus established when he said, "If anyone wishes to come after Me, let him deny himself, and take up his cross daily, and follow Me" (Luke 9:23).

God intends for those who come to Christ to become disciples. A person can be a church member in good standing and still fall short of being a true follower of Jesus Christ. This situation would have been unacceptable and intolerable in the first century. We seem to have lost the biblical concept of church discipleship and discipline and the true standards of what it means to be a Christian in society. And tragically, we have become so accustomed to this reality in the contemporary church that we have made ourselves immune to the facts.

The consequence that often emerges from these realities is that the church loses its vibrant identity as the body of Christ. This can be most serious, even tragic. When church growth fails to be true kingdom discipleship growth, we lose the kingdom perspective. In addition, the church can slip into depersonalization and institutionalism. The church of Jesus Christ does not exist simply to boast of its numbers and influence. The church exists for people, and before God every individual is important.

Above all, the church exists for the glory of God and kingdom extension. If a congregation loses its identity as the body of Christ ministering in a kingdom context, it eventually begins to deteriorate as it grieves the Spirit of God and carnality takes over. That church ultimately has its candlestick removed (Rev. 2:5). Growth must be seen in its full biblical perspective; social dynamics must not become the controlling factor in seeking growth. Institutionalism is to be kept in its proper place. Reaching people for Christ for the glory of God must constitute the purpose for all God's people. Wherein does the answer to our perplexities lie?

THE ANSWER

Dr. Rick Warren in his book *The Purpose Driven Church* has struck the right note. He declares that *the spiritually healthy church is the church that grows.* Therein the answer can be found. A spiritually healthy congregation becomes the church that experiences growth with integrity. As Warren has said, you do not need to tell a healthy child to grow. That has been true through two thousand years of the work of the Spirit of God in the life of the body of Christ, and it stands true to this day. Church health and church growth go hand in hand. Churches can enjoy explosive growth when they are spiritually healthy.

GROWTH THAT LASTS EMERGES IN THE HEALTHY CHURCH

Several foundational principles surface out of the concept of the spiritually healthy church. In the first place, the healthy church becomes a church so permeated by the presence of the Holy Spirit that the very image of Christ is formed within the body. Paul prayed for the Galatians: "My children, with whom I am again in labor until Christ is formed in you" (Gal. 4:19). Beautiful buildings, a dynamic worship service, good community ministries sensitive to those we want to reach, and a thousand other aspects are helpful. But if there be no genuine moving of the Holy Spirit forming Christ in the body, then all that can be said about such a church is that it actually is no more than a good organization. The Spirit of God alone creates the church—the church in the full biblical sense. And he operates on the basis of a spiritually healthy body, and this means spiritually healthy believers.

The healthy church is a church given to the disciplines of discipleship. God is far more concerned about our intimate walk with Jesus Christ than he is about many things that we think are so important in church life and service. In the final analysis, a healthy church abides in Christ, bearing the fruit of the Spirit. Again to the Galatians, Paul wrote, "The fruit of the Spirit is love, joy, peace, patience, kindness, goodness, faithfulness, gentleness, self-control; against such things there is no law" (Gal. 5:22–23). Clearly, the primary fruit of the Spirit is love. A fruit-bearing believer loves God and loves one's neighbor as one's self. This means there will be service for Christ to others because love demands such (1 John 3:17–18).

In a word, the spiritually healthy church becomes a congregation where the Spirit of God governs and permeates every aspect of its life. This stands true individually and collectively in the body. In the Western world, we often neglect the corporate aspects of the Christian experience in our inordinate emphasis on individualism. No one denies that the Spirit of God enters every individual Christian and works to form Christ within that person, thus making him or her a true servant. Yet the Spirit of God operates and forms the church corporate into a true body of Christ.

This means the Holy Spirit must have complete control to govern, direct, lead, and permeate every aspect of corporate church life. Such makes for a healthy congregation. When this takes place, churches begin to see great change. The whole congregation experiences a reversal from mere culturalism to the church becoming the "salt of the earth" and the "light of the world" (Matt. 5:13–16), and this, in turn, impacts culture and ultimately changes society. This has happened in the past *and it can happen today*. That's a healthy body, and that means growth. Rick Warren had it right.

Let it never be forgotten that God truly does want the church to grow. The New Testament pattern has set the pace. The Acts of the

Apostles was penned by the beloved physician Luke to demonstrate that a small "Jewish sect" in a very obscure part of the Roman world had in a matter of a few decades grown into a worldwide movement that had the entire Roman Empire up in arms. That is growth, that is influence, that is power, that is God's way in transforming society.

Jesus said, "You shall receive power when the Holy Spirit has come upon you; and you shall be My witnesses both in Jerusalem, and in all Judea and Samaria, and even to the remotest part of the earth" (Acts 1:8). The mission motif assumes a central role in the Scriptures. God desires his church to grow and to see his kingdom extended worldwide. But a question arises in light of these wonderful realities.

THE CENTRAL QUESTION

We are thrust back to the old problem: Why does growth not always occur? Why do we seem to fall short so often? Why are we not the healthy congregations that God expects? When can we experience the explosive growth seen in the past? When can we once again see what happened in the first century, and what happened to congregations like the First Baptist Church of Paducah, Kentucky, in 1905? The answer is simple, yet profound. The spiritually healthy growing church becomes a vibrant congregation during the time of a *great spiritual awakening*. This truth constitutes the key.

EXPLOSIVE CHURCH GROWTH

When the Spirit of God falls in reviving, renewing power, great things happen. As the psalmist prayed:

O LORD, Thou didst show favor to Thy land;
Thou didst restore the captivity of Jacob.
Thou didst forgive the iniquity of Thy people;
Thou didst cover all their sin.   [Selah.
Thou didst withdraw all Thy fury;
Thou didst turn away from Thy burning anger.
Restore us, O God of our salvation,

And cause Thine indignation toward us to cease.
Wilt Thou be angry with us forever?
Wilt Thou prolong Thine anger to all generations?
Wilt Thou not Thyself revive us again,
That Thy people may rejoice in Thee?
Show us Thy lovingkindness, O LORD,
And grant us Thy salvation. (Ps. 85:1–7)

Therein lies the "secret," and it is no secret at all. Great growth—genuine, lasting growth—comes when authentic spiritual revival bursts upon the people of God. This explains what happened in Paducah, Kentucky, and this surely constitutes our essential need today.

Donald McGavran was very much alive to this fact. Picking up on the revival that emanated first from Wales in 1904 and then permeated much of the world, McGavran talks about what occurred on the Asian mission fields in those dynamic days. He said, "In the Khassi Hills . . . God had ripened populations. In them, when the missionaries and congregations heard the news from Wales and asked God's blessing and turned single mindedly to reaping, great church growth followed."[7]

McGavran then goes on to give a quotation from the pen of missionary Jonathan Goforth: "When God the Holy Spirit came, He accomplished more in half a day than all of us missionaries could have accomplished in half a year. In less than two months more than two thousand heathen were converted . . . then He came as a flood. Since then their numbers have increased manyfold."[8] We talk about the profound reviving work of God in Korea today. Allen Clark in his *History of the Korean Church* shared this truth: "Without question, the most important influence in the life of the Church, at this time and for many years after, was . . . the Great Revival . . . a movement that swept the country and affected the entire Christian movement as a whole. The origin of the revival may be traced to a meeting in 1903 . . . in Wonsan . . . in 1904 with even greater outpouring of blessing."[9]

The significant Edinburgh Conference of 1910 coined the phrase, "The evangelization of the world in our generation." Volume 1 of the conference report recorded: "By far, the greatest progress of Christianity in Africa has been achieved in the last decade [1901–1910]"; and that was the Holy Spirit's doing. McGavran brought it all together when he declared, "A movement of the Holy Spirit in the Church of Christ . . . thus depends on the initiative of Almighty God, (but) it is usually granted to those who pray earnestly for it. . . . The multiplication of churches nourished on the Bible and full of the Holy Spirit is a *sine qua non* in carrying out the purposes of God."[10] This is revival, and this makes the field ripe unto the harvest, and this spells explosive church growth.

Illustrations of this principle abound. The point of it all centers on the fact that the spiritually healthy church becomes the growing church, and the church becomes exceedingly healthy and vibrant during a time of spiritual awakening. Moreover, when a revival dawns on the land, *all* the churches experience great growth (unless they resist the movement and thereby grieve the Holy Spirit). And such quality growth comes to small, average, and large congregations alike, regardless of the social, cultural, or geographical setting. Further, the growth comes in a well-balanced manner: numerical, spiritual, and ministry growth. And that gets to the heart of what church growth is all about.

THE ESSENTIAL QUEST

Does it not seem logical, therefore, that we seek a spiritual awakening that will bring health and life and the power of the Spirit of God to the church? This does *not* imply that we should abandon good church growth principles, as we shall see. But let us put first things first. As is often said, the main thing is to keep the main thing the main thing. And the main thing centers on a spiritually healthy, vibrant congregation. Thus it goes without saying that most of our churches need a real revival. The wise church remembers Jesus' word when he said, "Apart from Me, you can do nothing" (John 15:5). Why not permit him to revive us? Why not, above all, seek him, his power and presence among us? This principle produces the essential thrust and theme of this book. Spiritual awakening and church growth do go hand in hand.

This moves us to the issue of what actually occurs during a spiritual awakening and how it relates to the enhancement and growth of the church and thus the kingdom of God. To that intriguing investigation we now proceed.

TEN QUESTIONS FOR STUDY

1. What constitutes the quest for church growth, and how did this emphasis begin in the last seventy-five years?

2. Give a definition of church growth and how it fits in God's kingdom.

3. Why is the kingdom of God significant?

4. Has the megachurch a role to fill? What is it?

5. What is the importance today of the different generations, and how do they affect church growth?

6. What cautions are essential to realize in the propagation of the gospel?

7. What are some of the realities to face in seeking church growth?

8. What must happen to a church to see it grow—and how does this come about?

9. Why does a spiritual awakening make a church "ripe for harvest?"

10. What then must we do?

CHAPTER 2

GOD'S SOVEREIGNTY IN SPIRITUAL AWAKENING AND CHURCH GROWTH

The last chapter concluded with the statement that if dramatic church growth occurs during revival times, we need to understand the foundational operative principles that surface when God sends a true spiritual awakening. Then we can grasp the full gamut of what actually occurs during such blessed times. In this way we can begin to fix our primary focus on those basic dynamics, infusing them into our seeking of church growth. This is a good strategy for kingdom progress. Moreover, God will honor such an approach to growth. During revival times great glory accrues to our Lord.

THE PRIMARY PRINCIPLE OF REVIVAL

The primary principle that lies at the very core of revival is a person: God himself. This is true because of the penetrating portrait of the God of revival that Paul paints. He described the Lord as "the blessed and only Sovereign, the King of kings and Lord of lords; who alone possesses immortality and dwells in unapproachable light; whom no man has seen or can see. To Him be honor and eternal dominion! Amen" (1 Tim. 6:15b–16). The hymn writer Walter Chalmers Smith expressed it well:

Immortal, invisible, God only wise,
In light inaccessible hid from our eyes,

Most blessed, most glorious, the Ancient of Days,
Almighty, victorious, Thy great name we praise.

In the light of these truths, the essential principle of real revival rests in the reality of God's unequivocal, immutable sovereignty. In every spiritual awakening, God's sovereignty immediately surfaces, and that in a brilliant way. He is Lord; he is the one who gives revival, and he gives it when and how he alone sees fit.

MOUNT CARMEL

The classic illustration of this basic reality is seen in the contest between Elijah and the four hundred prophets of Baal on Mount Carmel. In that historical event, Elijah threw down the gauntlet to the prophets of Baal with the challenge: "'You call on the name of your god, and I will call on the name of the LORD, and the God who answers by fire, He is God.' And all the people answered and said, 'That is a good idea'" (1 Kings 18:24). A fantastic drama unfolded and came to its startling climax with Elijah's prayer and God's immediate answer. The prophet cried out: "O LORD, the God of Abraham, Isaac and Israel, today let it be known that Thou art God in Israel, and that I am Thy servant, and that I have done all these things at Thy word. Answer me, O LORD, answer me, that this people may know that Thou, O LORD, art God, and that Thou hast turned their heart back again" (1 Kings 18:36b–37).

Look at the results: "Then the fire of the LORD fell, and consumed the burnt offering and the wood and the stones and the dust, and licked up the water that was in the trench. And when all the people saw it, they fell on their faces; and they said, 'The LORD, He is God; the LORD, He is God'" (1 Kings 18:38–39). The point had been made: the Lord, *Yahweh*, manifested himself as the sovereign God. Elijah did not create the fire; God in his sovereignty sent it. And revival followed.

Many years before this climactic event, Moses learned the same lesson. On Mount Sinai, another significant mountain peak, Moses fell into an argument with the Lord. Amazing! God will let us argue with him. But he is a God of grace and mercy as well as the sovereign Lord. At the peak of Moses' contest with God, Moses asked, "Whom shall I say sent me to those Israelites? They will surely want to know." And God answered, "Tell them I am that I am—*Yahweh*—the sovereign Lord, the Almighty has sent you." And the Nile turning to blood, the infestation of locusts, the hail and fire, the Passover, and the great Exodus—all these events proved he is Lord and does as he pleases, where he pleases, when he pleases, through whom he pleases. The sovereign God reigns. Though he always reveals himself as the "hidden one," he has bared his sovereign arm in all our lives, far more than we realize.

Therefore, we can confidently conclude that the power of a spiritual awakening rests within the sovereign Lord. There has never been a genuine revival that did not flow out of his all-consuming grace. And when God does bare his might, there can be only one inevitable result: *Growth*. This principle is foundational to all our understanding of spiritual awakenings and the relevant church growth that follows. But what do we mean by *sovereignty*?

THE ATTRIBUTES OF GOD REVEAL HIS SOVEREIGNTY

We will do well before seeking a definition of sovereignty to look briefly at the thought of critics who assail the concept. It should help us see what God is *not*. Today, some scholars argue for a limited view of the sovereignty of God. They put a serious question mark over his all-powerful, all-knowing, all-sufficient lordship. One such approach, perhaps for want of a better term, has been labeled "process theology." In this view of the divine nature of our Lord, a serious aberration of biblical theology exerts itself. This deviation takes its presuppositional lead from various considerations. The evolutionary hypothesis made its impact on the concept. Not the least of influences on process thinkers is God's seeming "inability" to cope with the perplexing problem of evil and suffering. This particular issue moved Edgar S. Brightman of Boston University many years ago to lay the early foundation stones in process theology. He projected the idea of a "limited God." Process theologians today take much of their que from philosopher Alfred North Whitehead (see Whitehead's *Process and Reality*). As leading process theologian John B. Cobb, Jr. confessed, "I became more of a Whiteheadian than [ever] before."[1]

Whitehead projected the proposition that God finds himself in the process of "becoming," much as we are. In other words, certain aspects of reality (like evil and suffering) God cannot quite handle at this stage. Still, Whitehead tells us, God is "growing"; therefore, the day may come when he can cope. At the present moment, however, God simply cannot fully and completely resolve all such problems. In a word, he sees God at this stage as *not* omnipotent, and his sovereignty as *not* ultimately all-pervasive. To Whitehead, God certainly is *not* immutable, unchanging. Consequently, final "absolutes" are virtually eliminated. Although these statements on process thought may be an oversimplification of the concept, they do express the basic thrust of Whitehead's approach and that of his theological kin.

Norman Pittenger of Cambridge University, one of the key leaders of this movement, devised his early thought system as a reaction to the extreme "secularized gospel" of the 1960s. This secularized approach was epitomized in the so-called "death of God" theology of Thomas Altizer and William Hamilton.[2] A reaction to that radical theology is surely in order, but did Pittenger go far enough? It seems he did not. He still wants to make peace with the secular, rational thinkers of the hour, and he does so in a fashion that compromises the biblical revelation of the nature of God. For example, Pittenger has said that God

. . . is always *related,* hence always *relational;* he is eminently *temporal,* sharing in the ongoing which *is* time. His transcendence is in his sheer faithfulness to himself as love, in his inexhaustibility as lover, and in his capacity for endless adaptation to circumstances in which his love may be active . . . . We live in a "becoming world," not in a static machine-like world. And God himself is "on the move." Although he is never surpassed by anything in the creation, he can increase in the richness of his own experience and in the relationships which he has with that creation. He is the *living* God; in that sense, we may say (as the title of a book of mine dared to do) that God is "in process."[3]

Although Pittenger's emphasis on the love of God and his benevolent involvement in the affairs and struggles of his creation can certainly be admired, his emphasis has drained God of his immutability. Pittenger has failed to grasp the *revealed* character of the sovereign God. He seems so eager to "resurrect" the "dead God" of the secular theologians and project God into the affairs of his creation (while making peace with the positivist of the day) that he does not see God for *all* he is declared to be in the Scriptures.

It goes without saying that to evangelize our generation, Christians must take into account so-called "modern man" as well as the "postmodern" mentality of the young generation. Gospel communication must address the secularized rational mindset. However, those who say, as did Paul Tillich, that "the Protestant message cannot be a direct proclamation of religious truths as they are given in the Bible"[4] are wrong. Although our "postmodern" advocates tell us there are no absolutes, God has spoken—and that in absolute terms. God's revelation of himself serves as the primary epistemological principle for understanding the sovereign God and his truth. *God does speak,* and he has spoken clearly in the Scriptures.

Furthermore, the Bible unmistakably and forcefully tells us that God is sovereign and immutable; and this settles the issue. Not only that, God's Word *does communicate* truth in convincing fashion—even to a secular world among New Age advocates. God is absolute in himself, and he reveals himself in absolute terms. And we can rely on this truth to strike at the heart of human need. (For further arguments against process theology and other views, see Appendix A. For a defense of the validity of biblical revelation, see Appendix B.) Now we must become more positive and see what the Bible—the revelation of God and his truth—says about the absolute sovereign Lord.

THE BIBLE AND SOVEREIGNTY

The concepts of God that emerge in the Scriptures form the definition of sovereignty. We call them God's attributes. Several of these divine characteristics, though well known, bear a fresh look in the light of spiritual awakenings. Three specific ideas are contained in three specific terms.

First, God is *omnipotent*—all-powerful. The Bible makes it clear that "the Lord our God, the Almighty, reigns" (Rev. 19:6). The infinite power of God was announced in his own words to Abraham when he revealed himself as "God Almighty" (Gen. 17:1). The Hebrew term is *El-Shaddai*. This designation indicates that God must be seen as all-powerful and impregnable. He stands incomparable in power. God displays his sovereign power in all creation. Thus, the writer of the Revelation exalted God with the words, "Worthy art Thou, our Lord and our God, to receive glory and honor and power; for Thou didst create all things, and because of Thy will they existed, and were created" (Rev. 4:11). The Lord added, "Is anything too difficult for the LORD?" (Gen. 18:14). Our Lord expected a "no" answer to this foundational question.

We also declare, as the Bible testifies, that God is *omniscient*. Everything is clearly visible to him, and no knowledge of anything exists that he does not contain perfectly within his personhood. The psalmist declared, "Behold, O LORD, Thou dost know it all. . . . Such knowledge is too wonderful for me; it is too high, I cannot attain to it" (Ps. 139:4, 6). God is aware of everything. He has his eye upon all things in the entire historical sweep of creation from the moment of the Big Bang until the new heavens and the new earth appear. He does not move through time and space as we do. God transcends time and space. Thus, everything for God is "here and now." He does not cognize through time as we do; he transcends it. Consequently, God knows all secrets, understands all our thoughts, realizes our limitations, sees our troubles, uncovers our sin, recognizes our faith, and determines our destiny from before the "foundation of the world" (Eph. 1:4). Only absolute sovereignty could have this attribute.

Finally, we say that God is *omnipresent*. God must never be seen as a "localized" God. This is why idolatry—which limits his presence—stands as such an affront to God. He stands infinitely above the tribal deities which the Bible condemns. Just as he knows all about us, we can never escape his presence. He is everywhere at all times. The Bible says:

Where can I go from Thy Spirit?
Or where can I flee from Thy presence?
If I ascend to heaven, Thou art there;
If I make my bed in Sheol, behold, Thou art there.
If I take the wings of the dawn,
If I dwell in the remotest part of the sea,
Even there Thy hand will lead me,
And Thy right hand will lay hold of me.
(Ps. 139:7–10)

As Frances Schaffer put it, he is "The God Who Is There"—everywhere one turns. God transcends our limited four-dimensional world of length, breadth, depth, and time. In the mystery of God's ultimacy, he stands above the world in his utter transcendence; yet he is always near (Acts 17:27). He encompasses dimensions far beyond ours as even quantum physics is beginning to realize. Although he is in and through all, he certainly exists beyond the physical world. The Bible describes him as "the high and exalted One who lives forever" (Isa. 57:15).

HOLINESS

Beyond the three key terms we attribute to God, God is absolutely, unequivocally *holy*. He calls himself "the Holy One of Israel" (Isa. 30:15). One theologian has called him "the Holy Other." Although we might not agree with all that neoorthodox thinkers teach on this point, we must agree that on this issue they are absolutely on target. If we should see God (which is impossible in this temporal life), the one overwhelming attribute that would fill us with awe would be his consuming holiness.

Remember Moses on the holy mount? He was distraught. He cried out for a fresh vision of God. He pleaded, "Show me Thy glory" (Exod. 33:18). God answered, saying that no one could see the Lord and live. Yet, God graciously said, he would cause all his glory to pass before Moses. And as he passed by, he promised Moses he would place him in the cleft of the rock, put his hand over Moses' face lest he look upon the Lord and be consumed. Moses would see the holy God with a backward glance as he vanished into the *shekinah* cloud of his glory.

When Moses came down from that incredible encounter with the God of awesome holiness and the Israelites saw him, they shrank back in fear. Moses didn't know it, but the skin of his face was glowing from his fleeting backward glimpse of God who "is light, and in Him there is no darkness at all" (1 John 1:5). *God is holy glory.* This attribute speaks of his absolute moral and ethical sovereignty.

All of this raises the question: Since God is this kind of God— omnipotent, omniscient, omnipresent, and consuming holiness— how can we encounter him personally, let alone in such a way that would bring his divine reality to our lives and our churches? God seems so utterly transcendent and so "other" that we could never "know" him. But there are other wonderful attributes of God that speak to this problem.

GOD'S OTHER ATTRIBUTES

Once again, as we turn to the Bible, the Scriptures make it clear that God is also love (1 John 4:8). He reveals himself as gracious and compassionate (Neh. 9:17), and slow to anger (Num. 14:18). In a word, God comes to us as a person who desires a personal relationship with us. Although he is sovereign and a God of utter transcendence, he also invades our lives in grace and mercy because we are his creation and he truly loves us. He displays a vital concern in us and desires a dynamic involvement in our lives. And "God so loved us that he gave his only Son" that we might have that relationship and meaningful fel-lowship with him (John 3:16). The sovereign Lord becomes the loving heavenly Father. Mystery of mysteries; wonder of wonders; but what a God of grace and wonderful compassion! All these attributes and aspects of God point to his loving, sovereign kindness.

GOD AND MODERN SCIENCE

The scientific world is beginning to recognize these theological principles. Thankfully, those in the scientific areas of cosmology, astronomy, and quantum physics are rapidly recognizing that if there were a beginning Big Bang (to which virtually all scientists are committed), then there had to be a glorious "Beginner." And that Beginner had to be one of infinite power, transcendent dimensions, and infinite wisdom and majesty. Cosmologist and scholar Dr. Hugh Ross has said:

The God of the Bible generated the universe transcendently, that is, independent of matter, energy, and the dimensions of length, width, height, and time. He personally designed and built the universe and our solar system so that life could flourish on Earth. Though the Bible does not identify the specific means by which God produced the lower lifeforms, it does state that He specially created through fiat, miraculous means birds, mammals, and human beings. Since the time these animal kinds were created by God, they have been subject to minor changes in accordance with the laws of nature, which God established. However, the Bible clearly denies that any of these species descended from lower forms of life. Human beings are distinct from all other animals, including the bipedal primates that preceded them, in that humans alone possess body, soul, and spirit.[5]

What a mighty God we have; what a "Beginner" he is! We can be grateful that the so-called conflict between science and religion is evaporating. True, there are those on both sides of the debate who still seem to enjoy the battle, but thinking scientists like Dr. Hugh Ross and theologians of mature stature alike are coming together, and the conflict is slowly dissipating. We should be grateful. Surely the hand of the sovereign God can be seen in this as well.

THE KEY QUESTION

The key question is this: If God is sovereign, the Creator of all, what does all of this mean as it relates to the church and its growth? Several things can be said. Primarily, it means that nothing exists past, present, or future that does not emanate from his sovereign hand. He is the source of all life and reality. God has life in himself and he gives life as he sovereignly wills. No higher authority, power, or principle exists that God must follow. He stands as the source of *all* that is right, good, meaningful, and enriching for life and vitality among his people and the entire universe. When he acts, his act defines the good and what is right. There are no principles of right and wrong that God adheres to. What God *does* defines the principle of right and wrong. He is sovereign and he acts as he wills.

If God is the sovereign source of all existence, and if everything takes on meaning in the light of his actions, then these realities become foundational for the life of the church. If he is truly sovereign, genuine revival *must* come from him. Two or three simple but profound principles for the church emerge out of these conclusions.

IMPLICATIONS

We must realize that if God does not move, there can be no life, vitality, or spiritual reality for the people of God. We may carry on the institution and go through the motions and even create a convincing facade. But if God does not act, nothing of any eternal significance occurs. Consequently, no genuine kingdom growth is forthcoming.

Another vital principle arises out of these facts: we, as God's people, stand absolutely and utterly dependent upon him. Consequently, faith assumes a vital role in the experience of God's people. Actually, the only thing that pleases God is our faith. The grace of faith becomes the channel through which his sovereign power flows. In this way alone, revival blessings abound. Thus, everything in the life of our church—not to mention our personal lives—should be based on God's absolute sovereignty and his mighty power as we rest in faith on his leadership, wisdom, and grace. And remember: God is holy love. Do we think this sovereign God will fail to act in love on our behalf and that of our church? God help us if we so fail in our faith. *Our God will work his purpose* through us. Take heart.

This leads to the issue of how God operates in sovereignty and reviving love among his people.

THE SOVEREIGN ACTIONS OF GOD AND THE SCRIPTURES

If God is all that the Bible and traditional evangelical Christianity have claimed him to be, he will speak to us and lead us. Human intellect, human striving, religiosity, and anything we can generate in our human strength will never be able on its own to hear God's voice and follow his lead in exploits for his glory. But *he has spoken*—and this loudly and clearly. The writer of Hebrews tells us: "God, after He spoke long ago to the fathers in the prophets in many portions and in many ways, in these last days has spoken to us in His Son, whom He appointed heir of all things, through whom also He made the world. And He is the radiance of His glory and the exact representation of His nature, and upholds all things by the word of His power. When He had made purification of sins, He sat down at the right hand of the Majesty on high" (Heb. 1:1–3).

God has spoken ultimately, finally, and conclusively in the Incarnation, life, atoning death, and bodily resurrection and ascension of our Lord Jesus Christ. To know God, to be pleasing in his sight, to serve him effectively and experience revival, we must know Jesus Christ. But this raises the question: How do we know about Jesus Christ and how to relate to him so he can revive us and use us powerfully in his church? The answer is simple and straightforward. We come to know about God's Son, his will and purpose, in the pages of the Bible. Through the written truth of the Scriptures, God leads us into the experience of the living truth, Jesus Christ. The Holy Bible stands as the foundation of all effective fellowship and service; and this relates dynamically to revival and church growth. The Bible becomes the source of all effective church life and ministry.

A HISTORICAL SWEEP

How our sovereign God has moved through the two thousand years of church history gives a clear picture of the centrality of the Scriptures. The entire Christian movement demonstrates that God speaks and acts through the body of Christ as the church lives and shares God's truth. From the New Testament we learn that the epicenter of the Christian movement—the main source from which the gospel went forth—began in Jerusalem and the immediate area. In the latter part of the New Testament era, the center of the thrust shifted to Antioch, where Paul launched his missionary journeys. In the next two or three centuries the main focus settled in North Africa. There, giants of the faith like Athanasius and Augustine arose.

It was not long, however, until that which epitomized the church moved into southern Europe. A division came between the eastern church and the western church—between Constantinople and Rome—and a curtain fell on Europe. After the centuries called the "Dark Ages," the gospel once again burst out in central Europe through Reformers like Luther, Calvin, Zwingli, and others. This movement spread through central Europe and into Scandinavia as the gospel was heard again in a powerful way. In the eighteenth and nineteenth centuries, the epicenter found its focus in Great Britain. The Puritan movement, the missionary movement, the great preachers of the nineteenth century, and a host of other tremendous advances took place.

It is no secret that in the twentieth century the North American continent became the focal point of the Christian movement as the gospel was sent worldwide through missionaries, the media, and a host of other methods. Now it seems that the center of the thrust of bringing the gospel to the world is moving to the Pacific Rim as well as the Southern Hemisphere.

In the setting of this two-millennium sweep of church history, the high points can be explained only by the awakening power of the sovereign God using the revived church as it moved forward in faith on the wings of the Word. Beginning on the day of Pentecost, we have a classic example of God in his sovereignty transforming the lives of a handful of people and through them spreading the Word of God, the gospel of Jesus Christ, in such a fashion that within three or four decades they gained the reputation of turning "the world upside down" (Acts 17:6 KJV). Only the sovereign God, by the Holy Spirit bringing the truth of the Bible home to human hearts, could accomplish this.

In the age of the Church Fathers, God in his sovereignty brought people across the scene to set the tone as well as the proper biblical theology to establish Christianity on a solid scriptural basis. This was unquestionably a sovereign act of God. Even in the Dark Ages, our Lord acted in sovereign fashion and raised up giants of the faith like Francis of Assisi, who was gripped by the essence of the gospel. And we all know the story of the Reformers. For Luther and others, it was *sola scriptura,* the Scriptures only.

Moreover, space forbids telling the story of the tremendous eighteenth-century awakening under people like John Wesley, George Whitefield, Jonathan Edwards, the Tennents, Theodore Frelingheusen, and others. Through them God in his sovereignty sent revival and transformed the church—and even the fabric of society—as they came to grips with God's Word. And who can attribute the wonderful nineteenth century to anything but the sovereignty of God? Kenneth Scott Latourette, the well-known church historian, called it "The Great Century." More people came to Christ *per capita* at that particular period probably than any other period in the history of the church, save the first century.

And so the story goes. God in his sovereignty has done incredible things for the life, growth, and advancement of the kingdom through his church. And God's great leaders based their service on the foundation of the Scriptures. What should be the proper attitude of the people of God who seek kingdom growth in the light of all this? The question demands an answer; but first, a word of caution.

A CAUTION

We find it easy to take these marvelous, sovereign acts of God and the truth of the Scriptures rather superficially because of our familiarity with them. Moreover, we tend to focus primarily on the human side of the equation, slipping into what Stephen Olford calls "evangelical humanism." The point is not that God does not use his people or that we should not use the best means and methods possible in his work. Nevertheless, the sovereign God is the one who acts, accomplishing the task along biblical lines. Human efforts alone, if they are not guided and empowered by the Spirit of God and governed by the Scriptures, do not bring about true church growth. A proper attitude on the part of God's people about his sovereign acts stands vital.

THE IMPLICATIONS OF GOD'S SOVEREIGNTY

The first and foundational attitude that should characterize the people of God is a genuine spirit of humility and dependence. How easy it is to slip into the trap of taking credit for what God does as if we did it all by ourselves. We eulogize the great preacher, the superb teacher, the fine organizer, and the effective leader to the point that one wonders if God had anything at all to do with it. Humility and dependence should always characterize God's people. As Paul said, "May it never be that I should boast, except in the cross of our Lord Jesus Christ" (Gal. 6:14). God honors this attitude. God has said, "I will not give My glory to another" (Isa. 42:8).

Understanding that God is sovereign also makes us realize and assume the attitude as *servants*. The Bible declares that we labor as colaborers with God. What a marvelous position before God: his servants (1 Cor. 3:9). The Greek word that Paul used so often about his service to God was *doulos*. The term literally means a "bond slave" of Jesus Christ. At the same time, we must always remember that though we may sow or reap, God alone gives the increase (1 Cor. 3:6). Any attitude or approach that exalts self over against God's central role in the enterprise is doomed to failure.

A proper attitude of humility toward God's sovereignty and grace actually builds, inspires, and develops faith in God's power to accomplish the task. Realizing who God is and how he works through his people inspires a deep faith in his ability to accomplish his purpose—and this inspires commitment to his purpose and plan. It means submitting to his leadership, wisdom, and guidance, and trusting his power in faith to accomplish his work.

A proper attitude of humility will bring glory to God. This has been said often, but it cannot be emphasized enough. We do not build the church for our glory, but for God's glory. We are not to desire the power of the Spirit of God that we might be seen as making a great contribution to the kingdom and thus receive the plaudits. We, bond slaves of Christ, work for his praise. This attitude God always honors and uses to accomplish his purpose.

A spirit of humility also makes us recognize how dependent we are upon God's Word for wisdom, leadership, and effective service. Having outlined how God has accomplished his kingdom progress on the basis of the Bible, we humbly submit our service on that foundation.

A proper attitude of humility in the light of God's sovereignty, as we take our dependent role, will bring great growth. Such growth can be explosive, making the field in which we labor ripe for harvest. With this attitude, we will have the right approach and will walk in the Spirit. This makes us useable in God's hands. Such an attitude and spirit should permeate the entire congregation. Happy is the church that has a proper attitude of dependence and humble faith toward the sovereign God, takes it proper place, and permits the Holy Spirit to do his work through the Word. This brings revival that leads to spiritual health and growth.

THE PRAGMATICS

All of this emphasis on God's sovereignty does not imply that we should cultivate a spirit of resignation and just "sit back" as we "permit"

God to work. There are many pragmatic principles in the Bible that thrust us into action. One thing a church should do is *prioritize* its service. Every congregation should devise a mission or purpose statement that will become the guiding principle of all it does. In this way a proper system of priorities can be created and the church can develop its programs on that basis. This takes time, effort, thoughtfulness, investigation, doing demographics, and a host of other practical actions that church growth advocates recommend. Only so much time exists, with a limited amount of resources and people available to accomplish the task. Therefore, we must prioritize, release our people from non-productive activity, and help God's servants put their hand to the plow and make an impact for Christ. We will see this principle developed more thoroughly in a subsequent chapter.

The church that understands the Scriptures, assimilates them, lives them, implements them in a sensible, pragmatic fashion, and relies on God's sovereign power becomes the church that grows. To know the truths the Bible teaches and launch out on faith is essential for effective ministry.

As a professor of evangelism and church growth, I have several students working on their doctoral degrees. One of my students recently conducted a project with his congregation that was alarming. Using five questions, he conducted a survey of his people's understanding of some of the basic biblical doctrines of the Christian faith. Here is a summary of the survey with its five questions and the findings:

1. The Bible is totally (trustworthy and reliable; false; confusing; inspiration) as our guide for living (multiple choice).
2. Trinity means:
   • God expressed in terms of three relationships to man.
   • Three gods in one person.
   • Three separate gods but one purpose (multiple choice).
3. Jesus Christ is the best way God has provided for people to be born again (true or false).
4. Salvation is not complete without baptism (true or false).

5. The two ordinances of the church are baptism and the Lord's Supper (true or false).

Of the twenty participants in the survey, 25 percent missed question 1 about the character of the Bible as our guide for living.

The question about the Trinity produced equal results, with 25 percent of the respondents missing this question. The student purposely included "hints" in the potential answers so the question would not seem intimidating because of its subject matter. Even with these hints, one-fourth of the participants missed the question.

The question about Jesus Christ is even more alarming. One-half of the participants answered this question incorrectly. Whether these persons misread the question or actually thought in terms of Jesus being the best way among the multiple ways, it reveals lazy thinking about the nature of Christ. This kind of laziness leaves people wide open to the false doctrines and New Age thought which are rampant in our day.

Eight out of twenty (40 percent) missed the question that suggested baptism is a part of the salvation event.

It was a shock to this author to see 40 percent of the people fail to answer the question about the ordinances of the church.[6]

The results of this survey are alarming, because a church grows as it grows in the Word of God. A scriptural awareness forms the foundation for a spiritual awakening as well as good church growth methodologies. The sovereign Lord honors solid expository preaching, in-depth Bible teaching, and an atmosphere that puts the Bible in its proper place in the congregation's thinking and understanding. The church that would grow must be involved in the Spirit-inspired Word. This leads to a further look at the centrality and importance of the work of the Holy Spirit in the life of the church.

THE HOLY SPIRIT IN CHURCH GROWTH

The free moving of the Holy Spirit in the life of the church spells genuine growth. When the day of Pentecost came and the congregation was filled with the Holy Spirit, the people in the city of Jerusalem stood aghast at what was happening. Finally, they cried, "What does this mean?" (Acts 2:12). In that setting, Peter stood up and told them, "This is what was spoken of through the prophet Joel" (Acts 2:16). Such a situation always creates the setting of great evangelistic growth. When the Spirit of God in sovereignty courses through the church, then the Holy Spirit in his convicting power (John 16:7–11) reveals the Lord Jesus Christ. By the sovereignty of God, the lost are brought to faith in the Savior. No Spirit spells *no revival*—and no revival means *no lasting growth.*

CONCLUSION

The church must learn to follow God's sovereign lead and to *trust* God to do his great work. The Lord Jesus emphasized time and again, "Be it done to you according to your faith" (Matt. 9:29). What honors God most is our faith. We get the things for which we trust God, and we should trust God to reveal his will and purpose as recorded in the Scriptures and send a true spiritual awakening. If our churches would submit themselves to God, seek his leadership in reviving power, and then trust him to accomplish great things, God would surely do miracles just as the Bible promises. Then great growth could take place. That's the kind of a God he is.

The church that grows lets God be God. If we understand who he is and how he works, assume our rightful role, and permit him to be all that he is in us, revival will surely follow. This will create a field ripe for growth. We need to get these truths ingrained into the life of the congregation. But God is holy. He works in great power only through holy people. In a word, the church must be a *purified* people. We turn now to a discussion of this principle.

TEN QUESTIONS FOR STUDY

1. What does the Bible mean by the "sovereignty" of God?

2. What is it about God that makes him sovereign? His attributes?

3. What is the basic error of "process theology"?

4. What are the implications of God's holiness for one's personal life and the church?

5. How does God's sovereignty relate to revival and spiritual awakening?

6. How does God's sovereignty relate to church growth?

7. What is God's final revelation of himself, and how do we find out about it?

8. Discuss the historical sweep of God's sovereign actions.

9. What does God's sovereignty mean to you personally?

10. What are the practical implications of the truth of God's sovereignty?

CHAPTER 3

THE PURIFIED CHURCH IN SPIRITUAL AWAKENING AND CHURCH GROWTH

Tucked away comfortably in the bluegrass of central Kentucky is the little town of Wilmore. To see the community on the map will not impress anyone. Nevertheless, an excellent Christian institution that has produced Christian leaders around the world graces the community. All the locals boast of their Asbury College and Theological Seminary. It stands as an exemplary evangelical institution.

In 1970 something startling took place on Asbury's campus. On a Tuesday morning in February of that year, a traditional chapel service was on the schedule as the student body assembled in the college auditorium. No one expected anything out of the ordinary—just another typical Christian college chapel service. The talkative students sat waiting for the service to begin. The session opened with the traditional hymns, prayer, and announcements. The speaker scheduled for that service was one of the professors. That was nothing unusual either. The college required chapel attendance by all students. Possibly not all were enthusiastic about the hour they had to spend listening to a professor.

When it came time for the message, the professor walked to the podium, paused for a moment as he looked over the student body, and said something quite startling: "I have nothing to say today." When a professor has nothing to say, perhaps something unusual is about to happen. The silent speaker looked out over the students and asked, "Is there anyone here who would like to share a word?" Again, a pause. Then one of the young men from the student body stood up, looked around at his fellow students and blurted out, "I'm a phony." That got their attention. What could he possibly mean?

The student went on with something like this: "That's right, you think I'm a committed Christian. Oh, I know all the right religious words to use, and I've walked around the campus throwing them here and there. You think I have a real walk with Jesus Christ. But I have to tell you the truth, I confess, I'm a phony. My days on this campus can only be described as not having any spiritual experience with Christ at all." By this time, everyone had shuffled up to the edge of their seats. They had never heard anything quite like this before, an open confession to the whole student body. What could it mean? Then the honest student really gripped their imagination—and heart—as he went on to say, "But last night I met the Lord."

In that moment, it seemed as if God took the sharp, two-edged sword of truth and pierced heaven's stormy clouds on that student body. There came such a mighty rush of the wind of the Spirit that the students sat there awestruck. Many of them sank to their knees. Some actually prostrated themselves on the floor as the overwhelming presence of God the Spirit, like a tornado, swept over them. And because he is the *Holy* Spirit, those students—like the prophet Isaiah—experienced God in his holiness high and lifted up and heard the seraphim cry, "Holy, Holy, Holy, is the LORD of hosts, the whole earth is full of His glory" (Isa. 6:3). And like the prophet, they fell under deep conviction of their sins (Isa. 6:5). It marked the beginning of a move of God in profound spiritual awakening.

What empty seats remained in the chapel soon filled with students and others who had not attended the service at its beginning. The moment a person walked through the doors of the auditorium, he or she was deeply moved with alarming conviction. God had come and revealed himself in holy array.

The auditorium remained filled to overflowing twenty-four hours a day until the weekend. Hour upon hour the students lingered. Few had much sleep or food or anything else. The president of the college suspended classes as the moving of God's Spirit coursed throughout the campus. We might ask, "What were the students doing all those hours?" The answer strikes to the heart of the whole concept of spiritual awakening: It took the students that long to get all their sins confessed and forsaken and to find God's forgiveness. Actually, the lights never went off in the auditorium; students could be found there in prayer until the end of the semester in June. We now know the event as the great Asbury Revival of 1970.

REVIVAL MEANS PURITY

Notice how it all began. The revival broke when one student willingly and honestly humbled himself before God, confessed his sin, and put the matter right. In that way alone did the purification process begin. It revolutionized his life and then spread like the proverbial floods of fire over the entire student body. This constitutes the inception of revival, and this spells blessings untold.

What came out of the Asbury Revival can only be described as fantastic. For example, the students banded themselves together in small sharing groups and fanned out over the entire countryside, sharing what God had done in their lives, how he had purified them and set their hearts aflame to experience Christ in all of his holiness. Wherever the students went, "minirevivals" broke out. Blessings abounded in educational institutions, in individual churches, and in a multitude of dramatic settings. Many people came to new living faith in the Lord Jesus Christ.

Moreover, the students gave themselves to meeting temporal, physical needs. They would paint and repair houses of old people who could not afford to have the work done. They got all the shovels and brooms the small city had and literally swept the streets of Wilmore. It became a time of wonderful kingdom progress and growth. God had come. Everyone rejoiced.

Asbury stands as a testimony that a spiritual awakening always purifies the church, and this in turn precipitates great service and culminates in explosive growth. Simply put, the church regains its health.

In the final analysis, the only impediment to spiritual health in the life of any congregation is the ancient and persistent problem of *sin*. Get that problem properly dealt with, and any church will grow. That is a good place to start if we desire true kingdom extension—dealing with the sin problem.

THE PROBLEM OF SIN

There are many reasons why sin becomes such a devastating impediment to the health of the church. Sin grieves the Holy Spirit (Eph. 4:30). And when he is grieved, he does not work in manifest power. It "quenches" him (1 Thess. 5:19). This fact can be seen in God's dealings with his people during the reign of Ahaz, king of Israel. The Jews suffered severely for their spiritual abandonment of the lordship of God. In those bleak days Isaiah prophesied:

"An ox knows its owner, And a donkey its master's manger, But Israel does not know, My people do not understand." Alas, sinful nation, People weighed down with iniquity, Offspring of evildoers, Sons who act corruptly! They have abandoned the LORD, They have despised the Holy One of Israel, They have turned away from Him. Where will you be stricken again, As you continue in your rebellion? The whole head is sick, And the whole heart is faint. From the sole of the foot even to the head There is nothing sound in it, Only bruises, welts, and raw wounds, Not pressed out or bandaged, Nor softened with oil. Your land is desolate, Your cities are burned with fire, Your fields—strangers are devouring them in your presence; It is desolation, as overthrown by strangers. (Isa. 1:3–7)

What a sad situation. Is there any hope? Then, right at that dark hour, a stroke of God's sovereign purpose removed King Ahaz from the scene and Hezekiah, his son, ascended the throne. Remember, God never promises judgment without also offering grace and mercy. On rare occasions, of course, God does "give up" on people who persist in rebellion (Rom. 1:24–26), and judgment is then inevitable. But Isaiah reminded the people of the gracious invitation of our Lord:

"'Come now, and let us reason together,' Says the LORD, 'Though your sins are as scarlet, They will be as white as snow; Though they are red like crimson, They will be like wool. If you consent and obey, You will eat the best of the land'" (Isa. 1:18–19).

Young King Hezekiah came to the throne as a consecrated, revived man of God. In 2 Chronicles the writer recorded of the new king, "He did right in the sight of the LORD, according to all that his father David had done" (29:2). And by God's grace, the Spirit used him to bring about the kind of repentance, reform, and renewal that Israel longed to see. Hezekiah walked in the fear of the Lord, yielded, and dedicated with his sins put right, and revival came to the entire nation. Israel in a real sense was reborn, and the nation found grace rather than judgment. That's revival. And it always unfolds with an honest revived person or persons whom God can use to bring blessings to many others. But what if a church suffers such spiritual sickness that no voice is raised—or if raised, not heeded?

The New Testament speaks a stern warning to spiritually sick congregations. In Revelation we have the Lord's severe words to the church at Sardis. In addressing this church, the Lord Jesus said: "'I know your deeds, that you have a name that you are alive, but you are dead. Wake up, and strengthen the things that remain, which were about to die; for I have not found your deeds completed in the sight of My God. Remember therefore what you have received and heard; and keep it, and repent. If therefore you will not wake up, I will come like a thief, and you will not know at what hour I will come upon you'" (Rev. 3:1b–3).

Sin so deeply offends the Spirit that he will not manifest his power and glory. Consequently, the church severely suffers, not to mention the fallout on the community when the church no longer serves as "the light of the world" (Matt. 5:14). It can be reduced to this: No spiritual power means no growth, and the community travels the path to destruction. The church must be spiritually healthy to see God work and extend his kingdom. The virus of sin must be eradicated.

SIN MUST GO

There are many reasons why sin in the congregation must be forthrightly dealt with. To begin with, sin destroys the godly image of the church. So often we hear the criticism that the church harbors hypocrites. We must recognize that as long as sin manifests itself in the congregation, this criticism remains valid and there will be little or no testimony to the power of the gospel. Hence, the church repels people from Christ rather than attracting them. In the first century, the church captivated people's imagination. They flocked to see what was happening among God's people. They stood amazed at God's presence and power among them. The believers lived in dynamic fellowship with their Lord. As Luke said in Acts 2:42, "They were continually devoting themselves to the apostles' teaching and to fellowship, to the breaking of bread and to prayer." The result was that "day by day continuing with one mind in the temple, and breaking bread from house to house, they were taking their meals together with gladness and sincerity of heart, praising God, and having favor with all the people. And the Lord was adding to their number day by day those who were being saved" (Acts 2:46–47).

People may be superficially impressed in their initial approach to the church and be taken with fine buildings, programs, and entertainment. But in the end, people come to church to *meet God*. What captivates them is the conscious presence of God among his people. This serves as the magnet that draws their hearts to Christ and changes lives. Unresolved sin destroys the testimony of God's people. It leads to a situation in which there is no conscious presence of Christ and real growth degenerates.

A BLINDED GOAL

Furthermore, when a church fails to deal honestly with sin in the life of the congregation, it blinds the church to the purpose and goal of its holy enterprise. It results in irrelevant activity and ministries. When this occurs, the church slips into the grip of institutionalism and loses its vital impact for Christ in the world. Those members who are willing to work often get chained to "nonproductive activity," as church growth expert Peter Wagner states. Although there may be a lot of activity, little lasting fruit to the honor of Christ and the furthering of his kingdom results. So the church goes blindly on, thinking that all is well when the Sardis situation has overtaken it. The church may have a name that it is alive; but in actuality spiritual death has crept in and taken over. What a tragedy—to be dead and not know it.

THE LIGHT WENT OUT

The final judgment that can fall upon a congregation that resists the sin-purifying activity of the Holy Spirit was uttered by our Lord to the church at Ephesus. Even though the Ephesian church had a word of the Lord's commendation ("I know thy works, and thy labour, and thy patience," Rev. 2:2 KJV), they failed to realize they had fallen short of what the Thessalonian church had experienced. The same three words, *works, labor,* and *patience,* were attributed by Paul to the Thessalonians, but they had experienced the Holy Spirit's mighty power. Paul said of the Thessalonian church that theirs was a "work of *faith,* and labour of *love,* and patience of *hope* in our Lord Jesus Christ" (1 Thess. 1:3 KJV, author's emphasis). Those qualifiers, *faith, love,* and *hope,* set the Thessalonian church radically apart from the Ephesian congregation. After all, Paul said what remains as essential to spiritual health is Spirit-inspired "faith, hope, love, these three" and the greatest of the three is *love* (1 Cor. 13:13). When these qualities are gone, mere "works," "labor," and "patience" can be far from the mark.

The Ephesians had lost their "first love" (Rev. 2:4). Thus, our Lord admonished them, "Remember therefore from where you have fallen, and repent and do the deeds you did at first; or else I am coming to you, and will remove your lampstand out of its place—unless you repent" (Rev. 2:5). What a tragedy when the laboring church, because of sin, forces the Lord to remove its "candlestick." The flame goes out, the light dissipates, darkness reigns, and the church loses its rationale for existence. Sin constitutes a serious problem indeed.

A classic case from the Old Testament illustrates this purity principle. Joshua 7 gives witness to a near tragedy for God's people. The

Lord had given the Israelites great victory after the forty years of wilderness wandering as the walls of Jericho came tumbling down. They then set their eyes on the village of Ai. That should be a "piece of cake," they thought; the town was small. So Joshua sent out just a few of his vast army to conquer the village. During the siege of Jericho, God had told them to obliterate everything and to take no spoil from Jericho. But a man named Achan did keep a little gold, silver, and some clothing. No one knew about this, but when the two or three thousand Israeli soldiers attacked Ai, they were defeated. That little village threatened the entire Exodus event.

What went wrong? *Achan had sinned,* and this brought reproach and defeat to the *entire* people of God. That's serious. Sin does devastate. The people of Israel needed purification. When they got it by God's grace, Ai fell and the land of Canaan lay before the conquering army of the Lord. Revival and victory had come once again.

REVIVAL MEANS PURIFICATION

When an awakening arrives, a church experiences a thorough purification. Many principles emerge from this foundational truth. First, God reveals himself for who he is: absolutely holy. In the previous chapter, we discussed in simple outline fashion the attributes of God. Emphasized in that context was the awesomeness of God's holiness. And this cannot be emphasized too strongly. Whenever God reveals himself, he initially reveals himself in his utter holiness. This immediately forces the church to face its own faults, rebellion, and sin. As a consequence, the church is broken.

In the Welsh Revival of 1904, it all began in the broken heart of young Evan Roberts. While he was studying for the ministry in a small Bible college in South Wales, a Presbyterian evangelist, Seth Joshua, spoke to the student body. Young Roberts, along with his fellow students, was deeply impressed by the spiritual power of the evangelist. A local church had engaged Joshua to lead a series of meetings. One night Evan Roberts went to hear him preach again. In the course of Joshua's message, the evangelist cried out that God could mightily use anyone he could bend to his will. Those words struck Evan Roberts in the core of his being. Broken before God, he sank to his knees in that little Presbyterian congregation and cried out, "Oh God, bend me!" And God bent him, broke his heart, brought him to the place of confession and forgiveness, and then raised him up as one of the key leaders of the great Welsh Revival.

Evan Roberts traveled to his home church after that purifying experience. He spoke to the young people and a few others in the little congregation. Only fifteen or sixteen people heard him speak. He looked into the eager faces of those who had a heart hunger for God and said three things: (1) "You must confess and forsake everything in your life that is doubtful." (2) "You must obey the Spirit promptly." (3) "You must be willing to confess Christ honestly and openly." That night all sixteen did, and the Welsh Revival was born. But it all began when God revealed himself in his holiness and one young man was broken and cleansed.

BROKENNESS AND CLEANSING

How ardently God longs to see his church broken over sin and to experience his forgiveness and cleansing. So often, particularly in our contemporary culture, we have become oblivious to the deadly seriousness of a wayward people and their lack of spiritual power. Our prayer should be that God will reveal himself and break the church. We need to be led into something of a "solemn assembly," permitting God to speak in his holy power to hearts that are open and hungry for him. We thank God that in some places solemn assemblies are being held. These can lay a foundation for a purified church that can open the floodgates of glory and growth. This is a church growth method that many congregations would be wise to use. It gets to the heart of the most serious impediment to the expanding church.

Several issues come to the forefront in the context of brokenness over sin. One of the keys is that complete confession must always be made to God. John tells us, "If we confess our sins, He is faithful and righteous to forgive us our sins and to cleanse us from all unrighteousness" (1 John 1:9). Every known sin, regardless of how small it may seem, ought to break our hearts and move us to bring these transgressions before God.

Another principle is that we should make restitution to those whom we may have sinned against. In the Sermon on the Mount, Jesus said, "If therefore you are presenting your offering at the altar, and there remember that your brother has something against you, leave your offering there before the altar, and go your way; first be reconciled to your brother, and then come and present your offering" (Matt. 5:23–24). There are times when it becomes necessary to confess, make restitution, and put things right with others. We cannot escape the fact that this is what Jesus urged his people to do.

The third aspect of confession was expressed by James in his short Epistle. He declared, "Therefore, confess your sins to one another, and pray for one another, so that you may be healed. The effective prayer of a righteous man can accomplish much" (James 5:16). There are even some sins that require public confession. We must be careful, however, and not push this principle to the extreme, as some have done. Confession must be made in the realm and area of the offense. Still, there may be times when it becomes necessary for honesty before a group or perhaps even the entire church. If sin has been a reproach to the congregation, it must be put right. Paul stated in his defense before Felix that he wanted a conscience clear of offense "before God and before *men*" (Acts 24:16, author's emphasis). This sets the pattern.

These exercises in confession should not be understood as nothing more than a psychological gimmick to rid oneself of guilt. Confession should come from genuine brokenness before God. Such confession should be led by the Holy Spirit for one basic purpose—the restoration of fellowship. John wrote to move us into fellowship with God and with one another:

What was from the beginning, what we have heard, what we have seen with our eyes, what we beheld and our hands handled, concerning the Word of Life—and the life was manifested, and we have seen and bear witness and proclaim to you the eternal life, which was with the Father and was manifested to us—what we have seen and heard we proclaim to you also, that you also may have fellowship with us; and indeed our fellowship is with the Father, and with His Son Jesus Christ. (1 John 1:1–3)

This seeking of openness and fellowship, as difficult as it may be, can bring about a spiritual experience that is vital to church life and growth. Fellowship with God is the ultimate goal of all spiritual endeavor. And dynamic fellowship with God implies fellowship with one another in the bond of Christian love. It even means being right with the community. This may entail restitution to the outside world at times. And if this is done, the community often senses the reality of Christ in the lives of believers and their congregation. Thus, the "outsider" may become convicted and drawn by the Spirit into fellowship with Christ.

Dealing appropriately with sin is no minor matter. It creates a church unified in the full biblical sense with a ringing testimony. Our Lord prayed fervently for this to take place. In his high priestly prayer of John 17, Jesus prayed: "I do not ask in behalf of these alone, but for those also who believe in Me through their word; that they may all be one; even as Thou, Father, art in Me, and I in Thee, that they also may be in Us; that the world may believe that Thou didst send Me" (vv. 20–21).

When the church becomes purified and unified, the world sees an embodiment of Jesus Christ. This convinces the world of who he is and what he can do for those who seek him. The magnetism of such a congregation touches the community and opens unbelievers to the gospel. What are some of the features of a healthy church that unbelievers should see?

THE NATURE OF THE CHURCH

The Bible presents the church on a twofold level. First, the church is a universal body of believers. Everyone who has exercised "repentance toward God and faith in our Lord Jesus Christ" (Acts 20:21) becomes a "member" of this universal body. This encompasses all the redeemed people of all times, races, cultures, and backgrounds. The Scriptures call this glorious, victorious church the "bride, the wife of the Lamb" (Rev. 21:9). Through faith in our Lord Jesus, we become part of this grand, living, eternal organism. The day will come when the church in this universal sense will stand before God as the pure, virgin "bride." What a day that will be!

Until that grand day comes, the church manifests itself in a tangible, visible, local establishment. Too often people think of the church as a building that sits on the street corner. But the building is no more than the place where the local church, God's people, gather. Sometimes we call it more correctly the "meetinghouse." A true church, composed of true believers, assembles together on the Lord's Day in the fellowship of Christ for worship, ministry, and the extension of the kingdom of God. Moreover, the church "scattered" in the world during the week is still the church. But whenever believers band together in an ordered fashion with some regularity and structure, this constitutes a local church or congregation.

Believers may meet in a large building, or under a brush arbor, or even on a street corner. The important thing is that they gather regularly for worship, fellowship, and ministry and then leave the gathering for service in the world. The body may wear a label like Baptist, Methodist, Presbyterian, Catholic, or Independent. What matters is that believers unite to obey Christ and worship him in purity of heart and mind. These truths mean that all believers ought to affiliate themselves with a local congregation. The Bible presents this mandate as God's plan.

The New Testament makes it clear that a negligent attitude toward the local church is a serious sin. The Book of Hebrews urges us: "Not forsaking our own assembling together, as is the habit of some, but encouraging one another; and all the more, as you see the day drawing near" (Heb. 10:25). All Christians must take this word seriously—and be faithful. God has assigned the kingdom service to humanity. We pray, "Thy kingdom come." The channel of this "coming" is a spiritually healthy, dedicated, purified church—Christ's vibrant body.

THE BODY OF CHRIST

One of the significant New Testament designations of the church, especially as it relates to service and ministry, is the "body of Christ." Paul told the Ephesians: "Speaking the truth in love, we are to grow up in all aspects into Him, who is the head, even Christ, from whom the whole body, being fitted and held together by that which every joint supplies, according to the proper working of each individual part, causes the growth of the body for the building up of itself in love" (Eph. 4:15–16). This passage portrays the church as a maturing, spiritually ministering body. This shows that God intends healthy believers to serve their Lord in and through the church. The core of the operation revolves around the inner working of the Holy Spirit who creates spirituality and purity in obedient servants. But in what manner are God's servants to serve?

SERVICE BY THE SPIRIT

Elizabeth O'Connor, in her book *Eighth Day of Creation*, tells the story of a person who saw Michelangelo lugging a huge rock down the street. The neighbor called to him and asked what he was doing struggling so hard over such a stone. Michelangelo replied, "There is an angel in that rock that wants to come out."[1] We, the church, are just a piece of rock, yet sculpted by the Holy Spirit through his sanctifying work. He chips away until he fashions believers into a beautiful body of Christ.

Paul employs the "body" metaphor in describing the church because of what a body does: It moves, functions, works, and performs tasks. Therefore, when we visualize the church as the body of Christ, we see the church in its functional, serving role. The Spirit of God purifies the church and sets the servant goal before his people. This involves some important principles.

DIVERSITY

A body possesses many parts with diverse functions. In like manner, a local church follows this pattern in its ministry. To force all members of a congregation into the same mold, doing the same thing in service, misses the mark. God intends ministries to vary with each member. Paul asked, "All are not apostles, are they? All are not prophets, are they? All are not teachers, are they? All are not workers of miracles, are they? All do not have gifts of healing, do they? All do not speak with tongues, do they? All do not interpret, do they?" (1 Cor. 12:29–30). The apostle declared, "For even as the body is one and yet has many members, and all the members of the body, though they are many, are one body, so also is Christ. For by one Spirit we were all baptized into one body, whether Jews or Greeks, whether slaves or free, and we were all made to drink of one Spirit" (1 Cor. 12:12–13).

A healthy, purified, well-proportioned body boasts a great diversity of members, each with different functions. The knowledgeable congregation recognizes and implements this principle. This diversity comes about by the bestowal of various "spiritual gifts" upon the people of God (1 Cor. 12:1). A pure, dedicated church fulfills its role as an effective ministering body of Christ. When this occurs, growth will follow.

UNITY

The church's diversity does not mean there will not be a central unity in the body. After all, the human body functions as a single unit. This principle means many things. For example, every member is equal before God. It also implies responsibility on the part of every member. John Stott reminds us, "The essential unity of the Church, originating in the call of God and illustrated in the metaphors of the Scripture, lead us to this conclusion: the responsibilities which God has entrusted to his Church He has entrusted to His *Whole Church*."[2]

The Great Commission applies to the *entire unified body*. The full membership functions to enhance the life and health of the entire church. The Scriptures present every Christian as a member of the body of Christ, each fulfilling his or her ministry. There are no exemptions. This makes for a healthy unity. The Holy Spirit does not create a body with lame legs or withered arms. The church as a diversified but unified entity fulfills its purpose when every member gives of herself or himself to worship and service. We are one in Christ. For any member to shun the call of service creates the need for cleansing and purification.

The church of Christ must also be seen as the church of the future. The Book of Revelation paints a beautiful portrait of that aspect of the Body. John wrote: "I saw the holy city, new Jerusalem, coming down out of heaven from God, made ready as a bride adorned for her husband. . . . And one of the seven angels who had the seven bowls full of the seven last plagues, came and spoke with me, saying, 'Come here, I shall show you the bride, the wife of the Lamb.' And he carried me away in the Spirit to a great and high mountain, and showed me the holy city, Jerusalem, coming down out of heaven from God" (21:2, 9–10). The church of God is the holy city, the new Jerusalem, the bride of Christ. The church will last in this context for endless ages. But this ought to be exemplified in the immediate, temporal moment. This comes about as the church is unified, purified, and fashioned into the likeness of Christ.

The healthy church is a church where love abounds. In the New Testament era, the people marveled at "how they love one another" (Epistle to Diognetus). When the love of Christ prevails in a local church, it becomes a glowing testimony to the world and it also focuses on ministry. The candlestick burns brightly, the blinders are removed, and God's people understand what church is all about. Its focus fixes on sacrificial ministry. This implies leading people to faith in Jesus Christ and nurturing the people of God into discipleship in Christ. This also means that the believer's devotional life of prayer, Bible study, and sharing will be exemplary. But how can this unity of love and purity be attained?

DISCIPLINES TO OBSERVE

Sterling spiritual qualities cannot be generated by human effort alone. For a church to come to grips with its sin and carnal lifestyle, as often stressed, God in his sovereignty must reveal himself in his consuming holiness. The church can only be broken as the Spirit of God comes mightily upon a people, revealing their spiritual condition and humbling them before the Lord. It all comes from God. No amount of human action in itself will create the quality of congregational life that will maintain the "unity of the Spirit in the bond of peace" (Eph. 4:3). This comes on the wings of *true spiritual awakening*.

But human factors do play a role in spiritual awakening and church growth. A number of things should be done to set the stage for a reviving movement of God. Through preaching, teaching, sharing, and leadership example, the facts of the holiness of God, the horror of sin, the need for brokenness and confession, and the availability of God's forgiveness can be made clear to the people. Everyone will not respond. Still, the remnant and the hungry-hearted people will arise to God's truth. The principles must be kept before the people. As this book develops, we will see just how these human factors come into play.

Another vital step is to keep the structured life of the church thoroughly biblical. Spiritual health comes through assimilating God's truth into the entire life of Christ's body. The Bible must have its rightful role. In the previous chapter we discussed the serious lack of biblical knowledge in some congregations. Scriptural understanding means more than giving lip service to the fact that the Bible is the authoritative and inerrant Word of God. It also means holy living on a biblical basis and service rendered in accordance with the Scriptures. The full truth of the Bible along with all its implications must be kept before God's people.

A third thing that has been neglected in many churches today is church discipline. In too many congregations a member can be guilty of almost any sin and remain a member in good standing. But the Scriptures address this issue forthrightly. The church has a responsibility to discipline seriously erring people. There is no place in God's church for open, flagrant, unforsaken sin. Church discipline is an important principle in the growth of the church. This keeps the church purified.

THE PRINCIPLES OF DISCIPLINE

The Bible sets out principles for establishing a program of church discipline. Discipline is not intended primarily to punish erring church members. To the contrary, the purpose of church discipline is redemptive. The restoration of members to fellowship with God and the church is the goal. The health of the congregation depends on it. Paul wrote to the Galatians: "Brethren, even if a man is caught in any trespass, you who are spiritual, restore such a one in a spirit of gentleness; each one looking to yourself, lest you too be tempted. Bear one another's burdens, and thus fulfill the law of Christ" (6:1–2). When a believer errs, a spiritual member of the church should lovingly attempt to lead him or her back into fellowship with God and the church. Jesus held up this principle:

"If your brother sins, go and reprove him in private; if he listens to you, you have won your brother. But if he does not listen to you, take one or two more with you, so that BY THE MOUTH OF TWO OR THREE WITNESSES EVERY FACT MAY BE CONFIRMED. And if he refuses to listen to them, tell it to the church; and if he refuses to listen even to the church, let him be to you as a Gentile and a tax-gatherer. Truly I say to you, whatever you shall bind on earth shall be bound in heaven; and whatever you loose on earth shall be loosed in heaven." (Matt. 18:15–18)

An individual should first be admonished and helped by an individual, but if that person's word fails, two or three spiritual members should go to the erring brother or sister. If this brings no repentance, the entire church must become involved and discipline the person. Of course, such action is necessary in the case of blatant sin that brings reproach on the name of Christ and his church.

THE ESSENCE OF DISCIPLINE

What constitutes the actual nature of such discipline? The Scriptures do not present a detailed description. It might mean taking away the right to observe the Lord's Supper, in light of the fact that the Supper speaks of fellowship and communion with the Lord and one another. If anyone takes the Lord's Supper in a wrong spirit and manner, as Paul said to the Corinthians, he "eats and drinks judgment to himself" (1 Cor. 11:29). It might mean excommunication in some cases. The point is that everything should be done in the spirit of

Christ for the purpose of restoration and redemption. The discipline should be in direct proportion to the offense.

Of course, it could be that the offending church member does not know Jesus Christ at all. Many members in the average church show few signs of the regenerating power of Christ in their lives. Evangelist Billy Graham said that one of the greatest evangelistic opportunities today is the organized church itself. Appropriate discipline might lead such people to genuine repentance and faith in the salvation work of the Lord Jesus Christ.

It may be a large order to get a program of church discipline established. The principle has been a muted issue for decades, although church discipline in the past was a common practice. It would be wise to proceed with caution and with much instruction and prayer so the people will understand the purpose and goal of church discipline.

What does discipline have to do with church growth? Discipline aids in the purification process. As we have emphasized again and again, sin among the people of God grieves the Spirit. This hinders the moving and power of the Spirit, and the result is spiritual stagnation. The purpose of the work of God among his people is: "that He might present to Himself the church in all her glory, having no spot or wrinkle or any such thing; but that she should be holy and blameless" (Eph. 5:27). Although Paul in this verse was referring to the culmination of the present age, we wish to see the church moving to that goal in this time frame. Revival can aid in creating godliness and discipline. When these things come to pass, unity and fellowship with God emerge, and the church begins to make a significant impact on the world.

VITAL PRAYER AND RESULTS

This quest for unity and love and a purified church makes one thing central: *Much prayer becomes vital.* Prayer keeps a congregation humble before God, realizing its utter dependence upon him. In that spirit, God works. History demonstrates that persistent, prevailing prayer opens the door and invites heaven-sent revival—but more of that later.

WHAT HAPPENS

When true spiritual awakening occurs among a people and health is restored, several "new" things always burst in on a congregation. A new commitment to Christ grips the church. God's people present their bodies "a living sacrifice" (Rom. 12:1). The old hymn "I Surrender All" had it right:

All to Jesus I surrender,
All to Him I freely give;
I will ever love and trust Him,
In His presence daily live.
All to Thee, my Blessed Savior,
I surrender all.[3]

Such commitment opens the door for a vital program of spiritual, numerical, and ministry growth. This advances the kingdom of Christ.

Then a new zeal begins to permeate the people of God. A real hunger and thirst for God's righteousness—yea, for God himself—develops. What God wishes to see in his people is a hunger and thirst for himself. The revived, yielded, purified people of God long for the Lord. They seek the blessings of the Lord, and God graciously gives his best. But he wants us above all to want him. God is more important by far than even his blessings. When revival comes, God becomes paramount and "all in all" to his people. And they will not be disappointed. As Jesus said, "Blessed are those who hunger and thirst for righteousness, for they shall be satisfied" (Matt. 5:6).

Finally, the awakened, purified church sacrifices all for God's praise. And this is truly "new" for many believers. But this spirit wins the day, no matter the depth of the sacrifice. A committed, revived Christian pastor in Africa was martyred for his faith. He paid the supreme price with his own blood for the cause of Christ and the extension of God's kingdom. Before his death, however, he wrote these words:

I'm part of the fellowship of the unashamed. I have the Holy Spirit's power. The die has been cast. I have stepped over the line. The decision has been made. I'm a disciple of His. I won't look back, let up, slow down, back away, or be still. My past is redeemed, my present makes sense, my future is secure. I'm finished and done with low living, sight walking, smooth knees, colorless dreams, tamed visions, worldly talking, cheap giving and dwarfed goals.

I no longer need preeminence, prosperity, position, promotions, plaudits, or popularity. I don't have to be right, first, tops, recognized, praised, regarded or rewarded. I now live by faith, lean on His presence, walk by patience, am uplifted by prayer, and I labor with power.

My face is set, my gait is fast, my goal is Heaven, my road is narrow, my way rough, my companions are few, my Guide reliable, my mission clear. I cannot be bought, compromised, detoured, lured away, turned back, deluded, or delayed. I will not flinch in the face of sacrifice, hesitate in the presence of the enemy, pander at the pool of popularity, or meander in the maze of mediocrity.

I won't give up, shut up, let up, until I have stayed up, stored up, prayed up, paid up, preached up for the cause of Christ. I am a disciple of Jesus. I must go till He comes, give till I drop, preach till all know, and work till He stops me. And, when He comes for His own, He will have no problems recognizing me. My banner will be clear![4]

That is sacrifice; that is commitment; that is zeal and prioritizing that brings purity of life and great glory to God.

CONCLUSION

It should now be evident that the purified, loving, revived church stands on the verge of great advance and growth. It moves forward in godly discipleship. It takes great strides in evangelism. And it stands as a resource in the community to meet the pressing needs of people. Each one of these salient points will be elaborated more fully as the pages of this book unfold. But let it be said at this point that the purified church can only be described as a spiritually awakened church. May God grant us understanding to put the priorities where they belong as we seek to extend God's kingdom through the growth of our local congregations.

TEN QUESTIONS FOR STUDY

1. What is the first step in experiencing a true revival?
2. How does purity contribute to a healthy church?
3. How does revival bring about purity?
4. How are we made aware of our sins?
5. How does a Christian—and a church—deal with sin?
6. What are the ramifications of confession: personal, church-wide, and societal?
7. How does the Holy Spirit relate to service for Christ?
8. How does service fit in and through the church?
9. What does discipline have to do with church growth?
10. What constitutes the one vital principle of seeing a spiritual awakening today?

CHAPTER 4

THE HOLY SPIRIT IN SPIRITUAL AWAKENING AND CHURCH GROWTH

New methods! New programs! New structures! New buildings! New ideas! On and on the list grows. It would be a serious mistake to think that God does not use new approaches and structures in the life of the church. Societies change; so should the church. But one basic thing must be remembered. As an anonymous poet put it:

A city full of churches;
Great preacher, lettered men;
Grand music, choirs and organs.
If these all fail—what then?

Good workers, eager, earnest
Who labor hour by hour;
But where, oh where, dear Christian,
Is God's almighty power?

Refinement, education;
They have the very best.
Their plans and schemes are perfect.
They give themselves not rest.

They give the best of talents,
They try their uttermost,
But what they need, my friend,
Is God the Holy Ghost.

The author of this simple rhyme hit the bull's-eye. Even as God has declared: "'Not by might nor by power, but by My Spirit,' says the LORD of hosts" (Zech. 4:6). This truth assumes a central place in the church of Jesus Christ. And it all begins on an individual basis. A fascinating story in this regard is recorded by Stephen Olford in his excellent volume, *The Way of Holiness*. In the mid 1940s, during a spiritual life conference at Hildenborough Hall, south of London, England, Stephen spoke and was significantly used by God. Olford tells the story:

At the end of that week who should arrive from the United States but Torrey Johnson, Chuck Templeton, Billy Graham, Cliff Barrows, Stratton Shufelt and one or two others. As was the custom, there was a testimony meeting on the last night. Then to close the program, I preached on Ephesians 5:18. God came down in power. Tom Rees said, "All who want dealings with God, who have not already come into blessing, go into the chapel. We are going to give Stephen Olford twenty minutes to rest." I sat there with my head bowed.

Suddenly I sensed a presence before me. I looked up and I saw this handsome, tall young man, Billy Graham, I can visualize him now in his light suit, sporting an impossible tie! He said, "Why didn't you give an invitation?" I said, "An invitation has been given. In twenty minutes I'll be meeting with all those who really want to know how to be filled with the Spirit. Why did you ask?" He said, "I would have been the first to come forward. I don't know anything about this in my life."

He was unable to stay. He was going down to Wales. We made a date to meet in the Welsh town of Ponytpridd, in Taff Vale, only eleven miles from my home, where Billy was having some meetings.

I found that Billy was seeking for more of God with all his heart; and he felt that I could help him. For most of two days we were closeted at Ponytpridd's hotel with our Bibles open, turning the pages as we studied passages and verses. The first day Billy learned more secrets of the "quiet time." The next, I expounded the fullness of the Holy Spirit in the life of a believer who is willing to bow daily and hourly to the sovereignty of Christ and to the authority of the Word. This lesson was so new to me that it cascaded out, revealing bright glimpses of the inexhaustible power of the love of God.

Billy drank it in so avidly that I scarcely realized the heights and depths that his spiritual life had reached already. At the close of the second day we prayed, like Jacob of old laying hold of God, and crying, "Lord, I will not let Thee go except Thou bless me," until we came to a place of rest and rejoicing. And Billy Graham said, "This is a turning point in my life; this will revolutionize my ministry."[1]

As the cliché goes, "The rest of the story is history."

THE HISTORY

Not long after Billy Graham had his encounter with the Holy Spirit, he received in 1949 an invitation from a group of Los Angeles laymen asking him to conduct a series of evangelistic services in a large tent pitched on Hollywood Boulevard. Several of the concerned laymen had been instrumental in an earlier southern California crusade under the preaching ministry of the well-known evangelist, Billy Sunday. But the Sunday crusade had been some twenty or so years in the past, and the men felt the time was ripe for another harvest.

God had called Billy Sunday to himself some years earlier, so they searched about for an evangelist. They finally settled on the young preacher Billy Graham, who was serving at the time as president of Northwestern Schools in Minneapolis, Minnesota. He had a rich background in evangelism through his work with Youth for Christ. He was relatively unknown at the time, but they invited Graham anyway. When the services began, everyone felt there would be blessings, but no one anticipated the avalanche of glory that fell upon that tent. It soon made the front pages of the Los Angeles newspapers.

From the human perspective, key conversions did much to publicize the crusade. Stuart Hamlin, the most popular radio personality on the west coast at the time, came into a dynamic relationship with Jesus Christ. He let everyone know through his radio program what Christ had done in his life. Then Jim Voss, "wiretapper" for the west coast godfather Mickey Cohen, came to Christ. Voss, deeply involved in syndicated crime and something of an electronic genius, was gloriously converted. When he walked the "sawdust trail," it made headlines in the *Los Angeles Times.* Then Louie Zabarini, an Olympic gold medallist track star, found Christ. All these conversions brought national attention to what was happening under the Spirit-filled preaching of the young North Carolina evangelist. Newspaper tycoon William Randolph Hearst ordered his reporters to "puff Graham." And truly, the rest *is* history.

The Graham epic demonstrates that whenever the Holy Spirit fills his people and awakenings occur, multiplied conversions ensue and the church grows rapidly. Luke says about the day of Pentecost, "They were all filled with the Holy Spirit. . . . So then, those who had received his word were baptized; and there were added that day about three thousand souls" (Acts 2:4, 41). It always happens like that. To keep this basic reality vividly in mind is spiritual wisdom. But what role does the Holy Spirit play in spiritual awakening that in turn creates a field ripe for the harvest? We have already explored the issue to some extent. Now it should prove helpful to approach these living truths in more detail and in a systematic fashion.

THE ROLE OF THE HOLY SPIRIT

The first major move of the Holy Spirit in reviving power centers in purifying the church. Any church that aspires to become a healthy, growing congregation must permit the Holy Spirit to do his sanctifying work. This needs no further elaboration, since it was discussed in the previous chapter.

Then the Holy Spirit comes and empowers the church for its task. Jesus said, "You shall receive power when the Holy Spirit has come upon you" (Acts 1:8). The empowerment of the Spirit of God stands as essential for ripening the harvest and bringing subsequent growth. And what the Spirit of God does in this arena is nothing short of miraculous. Experience attests to this reality time and time again. Probably no move of the Spirit of God exploded with more power than what took place in America's Second Great Awakening. This movement of God was associated with many personalities, but none ministered with more spiritual power than the former lawyer Charles Grandison Finney. It was said of him that "he probably led more souls to Jesus than any other man"[2] up to that time. As another historian put it, "He [Finney] spearheaded a revival in America which literally altered the course of history."[3]

The nineteenth-century evangelist tells his own story in his *Memoirs*. On the day of Finney's dramatic conversion, he relates how God not only saved him but also on the same day endued him with great spiritual power. It may seem a bit lengthy, but what a story he tells. Finney used the phrase "baptism of the Spirit" where most of us would use the word *filled*. But the important thing is that God endued his servant with effectiveness for service. Here is his account of the event:

> I went to my dinner, and found I had no appetite to eat. I then went to the law office, and found that Squire Wright (fellow lawyer) had gone to dinner. I took down my bass-viol, and, as I was accustomed to do, began to play and sing some pieces of sacred music. But as soon as I began to sing those sacred words, I began to weep. It seemed as if my heart was all liquid; and my feelings were in such a state that I could not hear my own voice in singing without causing my sensibility to overflow. I wondered of this, and tried to suppress my tears, I put up my instrument and stopped singing.
>
> After dinner we were engaged in removing our books and furniture to another office. We were very busy in this, and

had but little conversation all the afternoon. My mind, however, remained in that profoundly tranquil state. There was a great sweetness and tenderness in my thoughts and soul. Everything appeared to be going right, and nothing seemed to ruffle or disturb me in the least.

Just before evening the thought took possession of my mind, that as soon as I was left alone in the new office, I would try to pray again—that I was not going to abandon the subject of religion and give it up, at any rate; and therefore, although I no longer had any concern about my soul, still I would continue to pray.

By evening we got the books and furniture adjusted; and I made up, in an open fireplace, a good fire, hoping to spend the evening alone. Just at dark Squire Wright, seeing that everything was adjusted, bade me good-night and went to his home. I had accompanied him to the door; and as I closed the door and turned around, my heart seemed to be liquid within me. All my feelings seemed to rise and flow out; and the utterance of my heart was, "I want to pour my whole soul out to God." The rising of my soul was so great that I rushed into the room back of the front office, to pray. There was no fire, and no light, in the room; nevertheless it appeared to me as if it were perfectly light. As I went in and shut the door after me, it seemed as if I met the Lord Jesus Christ face to face. It did not occur to me then, nor did it for some time afterward, that it was wholly a mental state. On the contrary, it seemed to me that I saw Him as I would see any other man. He said nothing, but looked at me in such a manner as to break me right down at His feet. I have always since regarded this as a most remarkable state of mind; for it seemed to me a reality, that He stood before me, and I fell down at His feet and poured out my soul to Him. I wept aloud like a child, and made such confessions as I could with my choked utterance. It seemed to me that I bathed His feet with my tears; and yet I had no distinct impression that I touched Him, that I recollect.

I must have continued in this state for a good while; but my mind was too much absorbed with the interview to recollect anything that I said. But I know, as soon as my mind became calm enough to break off from the interview, I returned to the front office, and found that the fire that I had made of large wood was nearly burned out. But as I turned and was about to take a seat by the fire, I received a mighty baptism of the Holy Ghost. Without any expectation of it, without ever having the thought in my mind that there was any such thing for me, without my recollection that I had ever heard the thing mentioned by any person in the world, the Holy Spirit descended upon me in a manner that seemed to go through me, body and soul. I could feel the impression, like a wave of electricity, going through and through me. Indeed, it seemed to come in waves and waves of liquid love; for I could not express it any other way. And yet it did not seem like water but rather the breath of God. I can recollect distinctly that it seemed to fan me, like immense wings; and it seemed to me, as these waves passed over me, that they literally moved my hair like a passing breeze.

No words can express the wonderful love that was shed abroad in my heart. I wept aloud with joy and love; and I do not know but I should say, I literally bellowed out the unutterable gushings of my heart. These waves came over me, and over me, and over me, one after another, until I recollect I cried out, "I shall die if these waves continue to pass over me." I said, "Lord, I cannot bear any more"; yet I had no fear of death.

How long I continued in this state, with this baptism continuing to roll over me and go through me, I do not know. But I know it was late in the evening when a member of my choir—for I was the leader of the choir—came into the office to see me. He was a member of the church. He found me in this state of loud weeping, and said to me, "Mr. Finney, what ails you?" I could make him no answer at that time. Then he said, "Are you in pain?" I gathered myself up as best I could, and replied, "No, but so happy that I cannot live."

He turned and left the office. And in a few minutes returned with one of the elders of the church, whose shop was nearly across the way from our office. This elder was a very serious man; and in my presence had been very watchful, and I had scarcely ever seen him laugh. When he came in, I was very much in the state in which I was when the young man went out to call him. He asked me how I felt, and I began to tell him. Instead of saying anything, he fell into a most spasmodic laughter. It seemed as if it was impossible for him to keep from laughing from the very bottom of his heart.

There was a young man in the neighborhood who was preparing for college, with whom I had been very intimate. Our minister, as I afterward learned, had repeatedly talked with him on the subject of religion, and warned him against being misled by me. He informed him that I was a very careless young man about religion; and he thought that if he associated much with me his mind would be diverted, and he would not be converted.

After I was converted, and this young man was converted, he told me that he had said to Mr. Gale several times, when he had admonished him about associating so much with me, that my conversations had often affected him more, religiously, than his preaching. I had, indeed, let out my feelings a good deal to this young man.

But just at the time when I was giving an account of my feelings to this elder of the church, and to another member who was with him, this young man came into the office. I was sitting with my back towards the door, and barely observed that he came in. He listened with astonishment to what I was saying, and the first I knew he partly fell upon the floor, and cried out in the greatest agony of mind, "Do pray for me!" The elder of the church and the other member knelt down and began to pray for him; and when they had prayed, I prayed for him myself. Soon after this they all retired and left me alone.

The question then arose in my mind, "Why did Elder B. laugh so? Did he not think that I was under a delusion, or crazy?" This suggestion brought a kind of darkness over my mind; and I began to query with myself whether it was proper for me—such a sinner as I had been—to pray for that young man. A cloud seemed to shut in over me; I had no hold upon anything in which I could rest; and after a little while I retired to bed, not distressed in mind, but still at a loss to know what to make of my present state. Notwithstanding the baptism I had received, this temptation so obscured my view that I went to bed without feeling sure that my peace was made with God.

I soon fell asleep, but almost as soon awoke again on account of the great flow of the love of God that was in my heart. I was so filled with love that I could not sleep. Soon I fell asleep again, and awoke in the same manner. When I awoke, this temptation would return upon me, and the love that seemed to be in my heart would abate; but as soon as I was asleep, it was so warm within me that I would immediately awake. This continued till, late at night, I obtained some sound repose.

When I awoke in the morning the sun had risen, and was pouring a clear light into my room. Words cannot express the impression that this sunlight made upon me. Instantly the baptism that I had received the night before returned upon me in the same manner. I arose upon my knees in the bed, and wept aloud with joy, and remained for some time too much overwhelmed with the baptism of the Spirit to do anything but pour out my soul to God. It seemed as if this morning's baptism was accompanied with a gentle reproof, and the Spirit seemed to say to me, "Will you doubt? Will you doubt?" I cried, "No! I will not doubt; I cannot doubt." He then cleared the subject up so much to my mind that it was in fact impossible for me to doubt that the Spirit of God had taken possession of my soul.[4]

Evangelist Finney went out from that experience, left the law office, and began preaching the gospel with penetrating, persuasive power in the small towns of western New York where he began his evangelistic ministry. Entire towns were brought to faith in Christ. Such wonderful things happen when the Spirit of God in revival power falls upon his people for ministry. Although not everyone's experience will be just like Finney's, nor will all agree with all his theology, but the Spirit of God will fill any Christian who pays the price and uses these experiences to share the gospel and sing Christ's praise. In revival, multitudes come to the Savior, the church grows dramatically, and the whole fabric of society often receives a radical revamping for righteousness. We must understand that great growth comes "'by My Spirit,' says the LORD of Hosts" (Zech. 4:6).

LEADERSHIP

The Spirit of God not only empowers and equips the church for ministry; he *leads* the church into productive service. One of the classic examples of this is found in Acts 10 where Luke recorded the story of the conversion of the centurion Cornelius. This fascinating conversion story also demonstrates a fundamental principle of ministry and church growth. Cornelius was a God-fearer, a devout man, but he did not know the salvation that God provides in Jesus Christ. One day, in the midst of his devotions, an angel from heaven addressed Cornelius. The heavenly visitor gave him the gracious word that God had heard his prayers and that salvation awaited him.

We will do well to pause and hear what the angel went on to say. One may have thought the angel would tell the centurion the story of the life, death, and resurrection of Jesus Christ and call him to repentance and faith. Surely the angel knew that story. Angels know more than we know here on earth. But, the angel did not utter one word of the gospel. After the announcement that God had heard the centurion's prayers, the angel simply said, "Now dispatch some men to Joppa, and send for a man named Simon, who is also called Peter" (Acts 10:5). The angel then departed.

The angel did not have the commission to tell the story of Christ—even as desperately as Cornelius needed to hear it. The responsibility to bring the message of salvation, God has been *committed to the church*—as personified in this instance in the Spirit-filled man of God, Simon Peter. Cornelius immediately responded and sent for Peter. The apostle came and preached the gospel, and Cornelius along with a host of his household and family came to saving faith in Jesus. God gives the golden sword of the gospel into the hands of the church. No one else shares this glorious commission—not even angels. What a privilege! What a responsibility!

Another salient truth becomes obvious in the account of Cornelius's conversion: the Holy Spirit leads and directs the church in evangelization. This can be seen in Peter's vision while still in Joppa before visiting Cornelius (Acts 10:9–23). Apart from the Holy Spirit's leadership, wisdom and power, the church will make errors and may even suffer serious decline. The Holy Spirit must be given his leadership role in empowering God's people.

VICTORY IN THE BATTLE

Not only does the Holy Spirit purify, empower, and point the way to effective service; the Holy Spirit grants victory in the spiritual warfare of the church. Until the church of Jesus Christ recognizes the serious spiritual battle going on and engages in this warfare intelligently, little substantive growth will take place. Paul reminds us, "For our struggle is not against flesh and blood, but against the rulers, against the powers, against the world forces of this darkness, against the spiritual forces of wickedness in the heavenly places. Therefore, take up the full armor of God, that you may be able to resist in the evil day, and having done everything, to stand firm" (Eph. 6:12–13).

Being unmindful of the battle, we find it so easy to do the routine thing, keep the institution running and the machinery well oiled, never realizing that this spiritual apathy ultimately spells defeat. The devil is not necessarily vitally concerned about closing churches and seeing them eliminated; he is quite satisfied to see the church apathetic and refusing to wage war as the victorious army of God. But our Lord warned us that a battle must be fought. The path to victory is through the power of the Holy Spirit and the Word of God. In the Book of Revelation we read: "And I heard a loud voice in heaven, saying, 'Now the salvation, and the power, and the kingdom of our God and the authority of His Christ have come, for the accuser of our brethren has been thrown down, who accuses them before our God day and night. And they overcame him because of the blood of the Lamb and because of the word of their testimony, and they did not love their life even to death'" (Rev. 12:10–11).

The only manner in which "the accuser of the brethren" can be overcome is through the threefold weaponry that John described: the "blood of the Lamb," the "word of testimony," and the willingness to sacrifice "even to death." This does not describe a church at rest, leaning back on its laurels because things are moving along smoothly. Our battle goes beyond a little skirmish here or there; this is warfare to the death. Defeat is inevitable unless the church comes to grips with the issue and learns how to exercise the power of the blood of Christ and how to speak the word of testimony in genuine spiritual power. We must be willing by the grace of the Spirit to serve God sacrificially, even unto death. Without the Spirit and his awakening presence, we become inept in the battle and suffer setbacks, if not utter defeat.

But on the positive side, by the Spirit of God we can overcome. As Paul expressed it, "We are more than conquerors through him that loved us" (Rom. 8:37 KJV). A grand promise! Remember, our Lord said, "I will build My church; and the gates of Hades shall not overpower it" (Matt. 16:18b). As we go on the attack, Satan's strongholds (his "gates") will surely fall and we will conquer as God's victorious army. The world can be transformed by the conquerors of Christ.

A TRANSFORMED WORLD

The Holy Spirit works through the church to address the world and transform it. Initially, the Holy Spirit does a deep work of conviction in the lives of the lost. The Gospel of John expresses it in these words:

"I tell you the truth, it is to your advantage that I go away; for if I do not go away, the Helper [Holy Spirit] shall not come to you; but if I go, I will send Him to you. And He, when He comes, will convict the world concerning sin, and righteousness, and judgment; concerning sin, because they do not believe in Me; and concerning righteousness, because I go to the Father, and you no longer behold Me; and concerning judgment, because the ruler of this world has been judged." (16:7–11)

The Holy Spirit, the *paracletos* who comes by our side to aid and use us, does a deep convincing work, convicting the heart of unbelievers. He convinces the "world" of *sin*. Only the Holy Spirit can do this. Conscience may tell us that we have erred and made mistakes, but the deep conviction that the Holy Spirit brings centers in the fact that sin is a rebellious affront to God. There is a great difference between feeling guilty for some sin and sensing God's deep displeasure. The Holy Spirit alone can communicate these realities to the human heart and mind. Jesus elaborated on this truth by declaring that the root of all sin is failure to believe in him. Unbelief rests at the root of sin and becomes the source of all individual, specific sins. To convince a person of this from an intellectual perspective is practically impossible. But the Spirit of God, with the probing gospel, brings it about in powerful fashion.

The Holy Spirit not only convicts of sin; he also convinces people of *righteousness*. Jesus elaborated on this by saying that he was going to the Father and we would see him physically no more. While our Lord walked here on earth, he was recognized as the personification of the righteousness of God. All standards of ethics, morals, and right were personified in him. But now he is gone and we see the standard no more in a physical sense. Yet, with spiritual insight engendered by the Holy Spirit, people can come to understand the principle of God's righteousness in Christ and that God demands this level of righteousness in us. The standard is high—as high as Jesus himself. In a word, to be acceptable to God, a person must be as righteous, just, and blameless as Jesus Christ. Our Lord said that except one's righteousness exceeds the righteousness of the scribes and Pharisees, he or she would not enter the kingdom of heaven (Matt. 5:20).

From a human perspective, to scale the mountain height of Christ's righteousness appears impossible. Yet, the world seems to strive for such a goal. The great satanic deception of the ages revolves around the delusion that we can attain sufficient righteousness on our own to be acceptable in God's sight. All the world's religions base their doctrine on this principle, urging people to keep on trying. They fail to understand, as the prophet Isaiah said, that "all our righteous deeds are like a filthy garment" (Isa. 64:6). Only the righteousness of Christ is sufficient to satisfy a holy God. But how can we possibly attain to this level? The wonderful news of the gospel is that Jesus became "sin on our behalf, that we might become the righteousness of God in Him" (2 Cor. 5:21). By faith, God imputes—sets to our account—the righteousness of Christ because of his atoning work. In the annals of God's eternal book, we are accounted righteous because of our personal faith in a personal, crucified, resurrected Lord. God in grace has made his Son our "righteousness" (1 Cor. 1:30). Only the Holy Spirit can make this gospel truth clear and plain to people as they muddle through life, trying to create a righteousness of their own.

Finally, the Holy Spirit convinces the world of *judgment*. In a recent conversation Billy Graham said, "There is too little preaching today on judgment and hell." He even acknowledged that in recent years he had not emphasized these truths as strongly as he did in his early days. We seem to be living in a time when the old "hellfire and damnation" preaching does not strike a popular chord as it once did. Yet the Holy Spirit courses through the world to convince the unbeliever that judgment lies ahead. The writer of Hebrews wrote, "It is appointed for man to die once and after this comes judgment" (Heb. 9:27).

If this be true—and surely it is—then how vital and essential that people come to understand and "flee from the wrath to come" (Luke 3:7). The problem centers in the fact that contemporary society has developed a sophisticated, secularized attitude and lifestyle. The average person scoffs at the idea of judgment and hell. It does not seem "politically correct" to tell people that hell opens its jaws to receive those who reject Christ. Yet, it is true; people who refuse Christ's salvation go to hell. When the Spirit of God makes these biblical truths alive to the unbeliever, a serious sense of need often surfaces and the truth of Christ comes crashing through.

Thus it stands essential that the Spirit of God be given freedom of movement in our congregations to convince people of sin, righteousness, and judgment. In this way alone will we experience the kind of spiritual dynamic that moves people to the Lord and his church. This brings genuine kingdom growth. The Holy Spirit is the only one who takes the gospel of Christ, reveals them to empty lives, and thus exalts in real effect the Lord Jesus. In the Gospel of John we read, "He shall glorify Me; for He shall take of Mine, and shall disclose it to you" (16:14). As Paul said to the Corinthian church: "Which things we also speak, not in words taught by human wisdom, but in those taught by the Spirit, combining spiritual thoughts with spiritual words. But a natural man does not accept the things of the Spirit of God; for they are foolishness to him, and he cannot understand them, because they are spiritually appraised" (1 Cor. 2:13–14).

The Holy Spirit takes the sword of the Spirit, the Word of God as communicated by God's faithful witnesses. He lifts up the Lord Jesus Christ and instructs the "natural man," who understands little if anything about Christ. Then he draws unbelievers to the place of repentance and faith. The gospel is the "power of God to salvation"

(Rom. 1:16). In kingdom progress, the Holy Spirit serves as the divine "operator."

REGENERATION

When people come to saving faith in Christ, the Holy Spirit steps in and regenerates them. He gives new life. They pass "out of death into life" (John 5:24). The Holy Spirit takes up his redemptive residency within, making individual believers the temple of God (1 Cor. 6:19). They are set on the path to sanctification and glorification. How easy it seems for Christians to become so accustomed to these realities that they fall into the trap—as John Henry Jowett put it—of succumbing to "the deadening familiarity with the sublime." Nothing can be more sublime than to understand—and experience—the salvation of Jesus Christ actualized in life by the Holy Spirit. Our prayer should be that the Spirit of God will keep us alive to these biblical realities as he invades us afresh, reviving and renewing his people as he thrusts us out into the field that is ripe for the harvest.

This moves us back once more to the truth that in the entire process of salvation, the Spirit of God uses the church as his key agent in the work. The divine and the human factors are *always* there. Peter and like-minded believers become tools in the hands of the Spirit to implement regeneration, new life and revival, and church growth. If we desire to see kingdom growth, we must quit relying on gimmicks and "new programs" alone. We must seek the reviving, awakening power and presence of the Holy Spirit. How can we see the Spirit "released" in the life of our congregations?

HOW?

We address this question first on a negative note, although there are many positive things to be said. A church can actually inhibit the work of the Holy Spirit. The Spirit of God can be grieved into inactivity by the impurity of the church. Members who are not walking in fellowship with Christ and in the daily cleansing of the blood of Christ inhibit the moving of God's Spirit. The church on a corporate level can also thwart the Spirit's work. To ignore him and refuse to give him his rightful place in leadership and empowerment quenches the Holy Spirit. Perhaps the most common error of a congregation is to forget the Holy Spirit's presence and to build nothing but human structures. At times, an erroneous theology can thwart the work of the Spirit. Anything that deviates from the essential truths of the Word of God concerning the nature of God, what he did in and through his Son Jesus Christ, and the challenge to godly living and love that emerges out of these realities is heresy. The Spirit of God will not approve those things that pervert the basic truth of the gospel and godliness. Now to the positive side.

THE POSITIVE SIDE

Several things will release the Holy Spirit and his power. First, there must be a willingness to let God be God. The Scriptures tell us that God reigns as the sovereign, holy, infinite, ultimate, Lord God Almighty. We must let him be that in our lives and churches. The Lord Jesus Christ is the head of the church, and he must be given his rightful place. God's essential nature and Christ's lordship demand a committal and surrender to him through the Holy Spirit in all things in the life of the body. The triune God must rule.

Beyond this, a quest for a developing spirituality in the life of the church takes on essential importance. Our Lord expressed this in the discourse recorded in John 15. Jesus gave the disciples the wonderful promise of verse 3: "You are already clean because of the word which I have spoken to you." Then he went on to admonish those who had found his cleansing power in their lives:

"Abide in Me, and I in you. As the branch cannot bear
fruit of itself, unless it abides in the vine, so neither can you,
unless you abide in Me. I am the vine, you are the branches;
he who abides in Me, and I in him, he bears much fruit; for
apart from Me you can do nothing. If anyone does not abide
in Me, he is thrown away as a branch, and dries up; and they
gather them, and cast them into the fire, and they are burned.

If you abide in Me, and My words abide in you, ask whatever you wish, and it shall be done for you. By this is My Father glorified, that you bear much fruit, and so prove to be My disciples." (John 15:4–8)

In this passage, Jesus declared that a developing spirituality, based on abiding in him, will continually bear fruit and bring glory to God in the life of any congregation. And this discipline is generated by the Holy Spirit. Jesus made it clear when he said, "The Holy Spirit, whom the Father will send in My name, He will teach you all things, and bring to your remembrance all that I said to you" (John 14:26). An abiding discipleship lays the foundation for an effective life and church.

THE MEANING AND IMPORTANCE OF COMMITMENT

Commitment to Christ centers in surrender to the Savior day by day. As the apostle Paul admonishes us: "I urge you therefore, brethren, by the mercies of God, to present your bodies a living and holy sacrifice, acceptable to God, which is your spiritual service of worship. And do not be conformed to this world, but be transformed by the renewing of your mind, that you may prove what the will of God is, that which is good and acceptable and perfect" (Rom. 12:1–2). In light of God's mercies, how can we do less?

It all comes down to this: We witness the release of the Holy Spirit when we surrender to his working and put our faith and confidence in him. This does not mean that we do not labor. Spiritual apathy brings no honor to the Spirit. There must be deep commitment and vibrant faith on the part of the people of God. They must trust the Holy Spirit to be released in the congregation so he can perform his reviving task. When the Spirit by faith is released, great things begin to take place. The released Spirit grows the church and empowers weak believers.

CONCLUSION

The Spirit of God bears fruit through the individual believer and the believing church. This leads to effective spiritual ministry and genuine growth. This leads to the next theme—discipleship and service in spiritual awakening and church growth.

TEN QUESTIONS FOR STUDY

1. Who is the ultimate author of a spiritual awakening?

2. Was Billy Graham's experience of the "fullness of the Spirit" valid? What about Finney? Why?

3. Discuss the role of the Holy Spirit in the life of the believer.

4. How does the Holy Spirit work in the individual personally and in the church collectively?

5. In what way can Christians experience victory in their lives?

6. How does the Holy Spirit transform the world?

7. What happens when a person is regenerated?

8. How essential is commitment to the Spirit? Why?

9. How is spirituality developed?

10. How does a person fit in the Spirit's plan to foster revival and bring church growth?

CHAPTER 5

DISCIPLESHIP IN SPIRITUAL AWAKENING AND CHURCH GROWTH

It may sound strange to say that what occurred spiritually in Britain in the late sixteenth century has extended into the twentieth century and beyond. Four hundred-plus years is a long time for any event to last. The movement commonly known as the Puritan-Pietistic Awakening can be properly classified as a Spirit-inspired awakening in the most profound sense of the word. Yet, when Puritanism and Pietism are mentioned today, they conjure up thoughts of legalistic "killjoys"—the Puritans, along with extreme emotionalism—the "otherworldly" Pietists.

Such an understanding is one of the regrettable foibles of history. Nothing could be further from the truth. The Puritan-Pietistic movement in its finest expression is defined as a joyous time of revival that gave birth to a Christianity of spiritual depth and tremendous church growth. Granted, some perversion of the movement occurred—it always does. But overall, the awakening was a positive, long-lasting contribution to the church. So significant was the impact of the reviving Holy Spirit that modern evangelicalism was actually born out of the movement's matrix. It warrants understanding because contemporary church growth has its roots here. As historian Ernest Stoeffler of Temple University put it, "The importance of the rise of Pietism for the Protestant experience in general has only recently begun to dawn upon us."[1] May the old light shine again.

THE ESSENCE OF THE PURITAN-PIETIST MOVEMENT

The English Puritan and the Continental Pietistic thrust should be grasped in the singular. Many modern historians contend this awakening is separated only by the geography of the English Channel and the temperament and politics of two different peoples. It can be best described as one great move of the Holy Spirit in revival. As Stoeffler states, "The fact is that essential differences between Pietism and what we have called Pietistic Puritanism cannot be established because they are nonexistent. The pressure toward a certain pattern of piety within the Calvinistic tradition (regarded broadly) whether in England, the Low Countries, the Rhineland, or elsewhere was basically the same."[2]

The movement had its birth in the context of a church in the grip of an inordinate quest for theological orthodoxy. "Correct doctrine" ruled the day. It resulted in the Reformation churches of Europe losing touch with the laypeoples' concerns of daily life. Leaders were answering questions that the average person no longer asked. It resulted in the church losing touch with the workaday world. Under these circumstances, "large numbers of nominal Protestants treated their churches with benign neglect, respectfully accepting them as institutions to which one turns to be baptized, married and buried, but which should not be expected to enter vitally into life's concerns."[3]

Like a descending fog, an irrelevance along with spiritual darkness settled on the established European churches. As a consequence, a so-called "Protestant Scholasticism" developed. It differed little in principle from the Roman Church during the Dark Ages, except in theology. The average person in the church contended that being a Christian consisted of nothing more than being correct in doctrine. Experience in daily religious life was all but laid to rest. The people "believed," but the spiritual dynamic faded. All this may be a bit of an exaggeration or oversimplification, but "spiritual and ethical sterility"[4] gripped much of the European Reformation church.

Then, just when it appeared a new "dark age" would descend on Europe, a spiritual bolt of lightning broke on the scene. Thousands were suddenly confronted with a profound move of the Holy Spirit. They cried, "Lord Jesus, I want to know you *personally*." What precipitated this pious cry that went up all over the Western world? What were these Puritans-Pietiests declaring?

THE CENTRAL CONCEPTS OF THE REVIVAL MOVEMENT

The prime point of the movement can be seen in the German word *Herzenreligion*—religion of the heart. The emphasis centered in *personal* commitment in faith to Jesus Christ. Faith became inward, experiential, and all-consuming. Although the movement held to a high view of the Scriptures as the source of faith, mere intellectual assent to biblical truth did not make for real Christianity. Christ strives to affect one's entire personhood in a personal relationship with him. William Ames, one of the first systematic theologians of the movement, defined faith as "the resting in the Heart of God." Another thinker expressed it like this: "In the heart . . . we may know God and the things of God."[5]

Jonathan Edwards, a great American Puritan, made a clear distinction between what he called a "speculative" and a "saving" faith. The former could be no more than an "assent of the understanding," but saving faith required "the consent of the heart."[6] He said, "True religion consists so much in the affections that there can be no true religion without them."[7] This approach by no means implies an anti-intellectualism. Theology—good theology—was very important for the Puritans and Pietists. But from their basic understanding of personal faith as a reaction to cold orthodoxy, real revival came. This can be seen in the key ideas that flowed out of this basic approach. Actually, the Puritan-Pietistic principles define the nature of a spiritual awakening. For these men and women of God, it all begins with the primary point of Puritan-Pietism: *the new birth*. This experience alone makes a person right before God and adopts the sinner into the family of God. They took Jesus seriously when he said, "Truly, truly, I say to you, unless one is born again, he cannot see the kingdom of God" (John 3:3).

Luther put emphasis on legal justification, and rightly so. This constitutes the theology behind the concept. The Puritans emphasized the necessity of *personal* regeneration and sanctification, and this also rightly so. A proper relationship with God is more than a theological, legal contract. The experiential element ascended to its proper place along with its theological base.

RELIGIOUS ENTHUSIASM

Even though "religion of the heart" assumed a central role in the Pietists' approach, they felt distrustful of excessive religious emotions. Raptures, visions, and "special" revelations were suspect to them. Pietism always heeded John's admonition to "test the spirits" (1 John 4:1). Following Christ meant bearing the fruit of love and obedience to God more than mere emotions. Herman Francke, pietist preacher and educator said, "Love is constant and unchanging, and is to be discovered by your obedience to God, and your patience under trials, rather than by your feelings."[8] Jonathan Edwards acknowledged, "I had rather enjoy the sweet influence of the Spirit showing Christ's spiritual divine beauty, infinite grace and dying love, drawing forth the holy exercises of faith, divine love, sweet compliance, and humble joy in God one quarter of an hour, than to have prophetical visions and revelations the whole year."[9] Bishop Ryle, an Anglican Puritan, gave a similar word of caution: "I know no state of soul more dangerous than to imagine we are born again and sanctified by the Holy Spirit, because we have picked up a few religious feelings."[10]

FELICITY

All this downplay of excessive emotions did not mean that dynamic Christian experience was stripped of deep feeling. Felicity, the joyous experience of walking with Christ, played an important role. The Puritan-Pietist Movement saw daily fellowship with Jesus Christ as the goal of creation. The Dutch Pietist Teellinck prayed, "Lord Jesus, thou dearest groom of my soul . . . when shall I be given the full privilege, to enjoy freely, and with my whole heart, how sweet thou are, my Lord and

God. When shall I entirely unite myself with thee?"[11] Such prayer appears quite mystical. Were the Pietists mystics? They were not like the medieval mystics, as Hans Küng points out in his work, *Freedom Today*. Still, devotional writers of the persuasion have captured the positive aspects of mysticism, being careful to keep those manifestations in line with traditional, scriptural orthodoxy. For example, George Fox, Richard Baxter, Jeremy Taylor, and others, along with a host of modern Puritans-Pietists like Andrew Murray, Hannah W. Smith, and Watchman Nee have excelled on this point. They have seen that a balanced felicity is important to dynamic Christianity. This leads into the next Puritan-Pietistic principle, and it brings us to the core of real revival.

SANCTIFICATION

Sanctification—separation from sin and to God—has always been emphasized by the Puritans-Pietists. At the same time, they attempted to avoid what mature believers considered a heresy—perfectionism. Francke wrote, "We are not and never will be entirely perfect."[12] They continually emphasized the "exceeding sinfulness of sin" in the light of God's holiness.

Thus, they emphasized a constant need for God's forgiving grace. At the same time, their religious idealism ascended to the highest order. At times some may have become somewhat legalistic. But we must remember, as Stoeffler reminds us, "the profound ethical sensitivity of Pietism, a sensitivity which in the Reformed tradition of the seventeenth century was hidden under the bushel of dogmatics."[13]

Moreover, Puritans based their ethics on the understanding of New Testament morality. In our present permissive society and postmodern denial of moral absolutes, this emphasis needs to be heard and heeded once again. This aspect of awakening we desperately need in our hour. May God come among us as he did in the past and revive us to holiness once again. Then our churches will grow as they have not grown in many years.

To sum up the movement, the principle of godly discipleship made up the essence of the Puritan-Pietistic awakening. We can conclude that when the Spirit of God moves in powerful fashion, discipleship in Christ naturally ensues. If a spiritual awakening does anything for the church, it creates holiness, godliness, and an abiding in Christ that brings about true discipleship and service. This, in turn, fosters growth. Discipleship means growth, and this epitomizes the Puritans and the Pietists.

THE GROWTH OF DISCIPLESHIP

It would seem wise to set out a simple definition of discipleship. The term is used so often today that it runs the risk of losing its pungency. Our Lord defined discipleship very pointedly in these words: "If anyone wishes to come after Me, let him deny himself, and take up his cross, and follow Me" (Matt. 16:24). This statement of Jesus is also reiterated in the other two Synoptic Gospels (Mark 8:34; Luke 14:27). In these passages our Lord gave us the essential principles of discipleship. To be a follower of Christ means commitment to the point of death. In commenting on this significant passage, commentator G. C. Morgan said:

Our Lord restated the terms of His discipleship. "If any man would come after Me." They all wanted to, they all loved Him, they all had affection for Him. He said, If this is so, if any man desires to come after me let him first "Deny himself;" and secondly, "Take up his Cross." Let us consider those conditions carefully. Denying of self is far more than self-denial in our usual sense of that term. Perhaps we may best illustrate it by declaring that we have no right to make any sacrifice for Jesus Christ which He does not appoint. When a man takes on him some effort of sacrifice, simply because he thinks sacrifice is the right thing, and does not wait for orders, he is as surely a skandalon to his Lord as when he does not deny himself and take up his cross at the command of the Master. The true disciple chooses neither song nor dirge, neither sunshine nor shadow; has no choice but to know his Master's will and to do it. If He appoints for us the blue waters of the lake and all the sunshine of the summer, then let us rejoice therein, and not vex our souls because we know no suffering and pain. If He appoint a via dolorosa and a sunless sky, then God make us willing to take the way, because the way is His appointment. We must be in His will if we are to cooperate with Him.

The programme of the disciple is expressed in these words, "Follow Me." That is, make the "must" of My life the "must" of your life. I must. Does not that mean suffering? It may, or it may not. Suffering is not the deepest thing in the "must." The deepest thing is this; I must cooperate with the purpose of God, whatsoever it may be. I must co-operate with Him towards that resurrection that means ransom and redemption. On the way there may be the suffering and the killing—there surely will be some measure of it—but the suffering and the killing are not the deepest things. The deepest thing is that we get into touch with God and do His will; and whether it be laughter or crying, sorrowing or sighing, the secret of life is to follow Him on the pathway of loyalty to the Divine will.[14]

This calls for a look into the practical aspects of how discipleship unfolds in life. The church certainly grows on the basis of a committed congregation, and no one can be a true disciple of Jesus Christ without giving himself or herself to at least five specific Christian exercises that we call the "disciplines." These disciplines are at the heart of denying self, taking up the cross, and following Jesus.

A HUNGER FOR HOLINESS

A hunger for holiness initiates the process of becoming a faithful disciple of the Lord Jesus Christ. In the Beatitudes, remember our Lord said, "Blessed are those who hunger and thirst for righteousness, for they shall be satisfied" (Matt. 5:6). This amounts to prioritizing life's goals and decisions. We deny ourselves in the light of Christ's lordship. Thus we "seek first His kingdom and His righteousness" (Matt. 6:33). Our Lord coupled the command with a wonderful promise. He said all "other things" will then be added to us. This hunger for God's best is foundational. The quest for God and his holiness becomes the basis of where it all begins. This goal assumes such an essential place in spirituality that the writer of Hebrews goes so far as to say that, without holiness "no one will see the Lord" (Heb. 12:14). So the first discipline of discipleship centers in cultivating a heart hunger for God. When this priority becomes primary, the other disciplines fall into place. Revival prioritizes believers.

This raises the important question about how this hunger for revival and holiness comes about. A divine side and a human side once again make up the answer. The desire for righteousness and godliness is spawned by the inner work of the Holy Spirit. At the same time, there must be a human response. To grieve the Spirit—to repress him, or ignore him—thwarts his inner work, and we go on in our secularized lifestyle. There must be an openness, a receptivity, and a yieldedness to his inner work. Discipleship begins in personal surrender to Christ's lordship spawned by the Spirit's work of grace. In the New Testament, the word *Lord* (*kurios*) is used far more than the word *Savior* (*soter*) in describing the personhood of Jesus Christ. In order for holiness to prevail, Christ must be Lord in every aspect of life. This defines the foundation of discipleship.

Another growth principle in a maturing discipleship and the basis for spiritual awakening is prayer.

PRAYER

Probably more books have been written on prayer than any other aspect of the devotional life. R. A. Torrey gave some helpful hints on prayer in his volume, *The Power of Prayer*. He used as a pattern the early Jerusalem church in their intercession for Peter's release from prison (Acts 12). The church prayed successfully on that occasion and actually prayed Peter out of prison. How did they do it? Verse 5 gives us the clue: "Prayer for him was being made fervently by the church to God."

"UNTO GOD"

Effective prayer is always "unto God." Torrey said, "I do not believe that one in a hundred of the prayers of Protestant believers are really *unto God.*"[15] We can find ourselves more concerned about our requests than God whom we are addressing. It seems so easy to string a series of clichés together that sound good but say very little. We must be careful of the "meaningless repetition" that our Lord warned us to avoid (Matt. 6:7). When we come before God, we need to be vividly conscious to whom we speak. He reveals himself as the mighty creator; the powerful Sustainer; the gracious Redeemer; the loving Father; God almighty. So we should pause before we rush into God's presence. Perhaps we should wait until we are ready to steal away, head bowed, and say, "I am not worthy." But the Lord Jesus tells us, "Hitherto you have asked nothing *in my name;* ask, and you will receive, that your joy may be full" (John 16:24 RSV, author's italics). *In my name.* This phrase is a key to effectual prayer. We come before God in Jesus' name. What does this mean? It surely means more than just tacking a pious phrase on the end of our prayers.

PRAYER IN JESUS' NAME

This principle of effective prayer is simple, yet most significant. Torrey tells us, "It means simply this; that you ask the thing that you ask from the person of whom you ask it, on the ground of some claim that the person has in whose name you ask it."[16] We have no claims on God. God owes us nothing, and we deserve nothing but judgment. In ourselves and our sinful weakness we really have no right to come before God at all. But in Jesus' name—in his righteousness, in his position before God as our interceder, in one who has all "claims" on God because he is the Son of God and Savior of the world—in him we can ask for anything. Expressed in another way, we are "in Christ"; and in him before God we are righteousness and can come to the Father through Jesus, who died and rose again to make us acceptable to God. As Torrey put it, "When we draw near to God in that way we can get 'whatsoever' we ask; no matter how great it may be."[17] In other words, we stand before God in Christ's worthiness and righteousness—not our own.

Therefore, praying in Jesus' name means more than a mere phrase. Moreover, we do not pray to the Father "in his name" (i.e., in the

Father's name), and we certainly should not end our prayers with a simple "amen." We pray in the name of *Jesus Christ,* who, because of his life, death, and Resurrection, has become our worthiness before God the Father to whom we address our praise and prayers. In the strong name of Jesus we can make any claim whatsoever, so long as it stems from *God's will.* This brings us to another prayer principle.

PRAYING IN THE WILL OF GOD

"In God's will" constitutes another vital principle in praying "unto God." Christian prayer is God-centered, not self-centered. It's not getting things from God; it's finding out what God wants and getting ourselves into cooperation with that. Prayer that fulfills his purpose receives an answer—"whatsoever" we ask. In praying to God for an awakening, the question arises, Does God wish to send a true revival here and now? How can we know? We discover the will of God in various ways, but the Bible stands as the primary source in discovering God's will. What does the Bible say about awakenings? Recall the prayer of the psalmist:

Restore us, O God of our salvation,
And cause Thine indignation toward us to cease.
Wilt Thou be angry with us forever?
Wilt Thou prolong Thine anger to all generations?
Wilt Thou not Thyself revive us again,
That Thy people may rejoice in Thee?
(Ps. 85:4–6 KJV)

This prayer comes from the Word of God. Therefore, it is a word of truth and authority. Such passages tell us that God longs to send a glorious awakening—contingent on his sovereignty—and bring about godliness and growth in our churches.

We can pray with assurance because "this is the confidence which we have before Him, that, if we ask anything according to His will, He hears us. And if we know that He hears us in whatever we ask, we know that we have the requests which we have asked from Him"

(1 John 5:14–15). Praying in the will of God, whatever the request may be, will lead to a confident prayer of faith.

THE PRAYER OF FAITH

The Scriptures place high priority on believing prayer. God receives honor when we pray in faith. Actually, unbelief is a sin because it raises a question about the veracity of God's Word. The Bible abounds in this principle. James said, "Let him ask God who gives to all men generously. . . . But let him ask in faith, with no doubting, for he who doubts is like a wave of the sea that is driven and tossed by the wind. For that person must not suppose that a double-minded man, unstable in all his ways, will receive anything from the Lord" (James 1:5–8 RSV).

To pray faith's prayer does not always come easy. Two things help us rise to this level of confidence in prayer. First, we must seek God's purpose in his Word. Then to know God's will, we should pray until the Holy Spirit grants the inner assurance that our requests are in line with God's purpose and God has heard our requests. "Instant prayer," contrary to today's prevailing psychology, does not bring many answers—unless, of course, an emergency arises. Then God surely has an open ear for our instant cry. But our Lord longs to have us come before him and "spend time." Perhaps the reason for unanswered prayers arises from the fact that we simply have not prevailed in prayer; we give up too soon. E. M. Bounds reminds us: "We are ever ready to excuse our lack of earnest and toilsome praying. . . . We often end praying just where we ought to begin. We quit praying when God . . . is waiting for us to really pray. We are deterred by obstacles from praying as we submit to difficulties and call it submission to God's will."[18]

The great Welsh Revival began (as do all revivals) by appointing a time of fasting and prayer. In that setting the Holy Spirit fell mightily on Evan Roberts, God's key spokesman in the awakening. That sparked the blazing fires of revival that swept up the Rhondda Valley converting thousands. The church grew incredibly. The key was that the people prayed until the answer came. They prayed with intensity.

WITH INTENSE EARNESTNESS

The word Luke used in Acts about the disciples' attitude in prayer was *ektenos;* it means literally "stretched-out-edly." The term portrays a person stretched out in an intensity of earnestness as he prays. This means that meaningful prayer comes from a burdened, broken, contrite, and agonizing heart. The Bible speaks clearly about God's concern for the contrite heart: "The sacrifices of God are a broken spirit; a broken and contrite heart, O God, Thou wilt not despise" (Ps. 51:17). David realized this principle as he prayed his brokenhearted confession in Psalm 51. He had the right spirit.

This type of prayer was offered to God when the Hebrides Awakening of 1949 broke out. The Hebrides Islands are several bleak, windswept islands off the northwest coast of Scotland. The spiritual temperament of the Hebrides in those days was appalling. Hardly anyone went to church; secularism and godlessness had become the order of the day. In one of the languishing churches, a small group of men became deeply burdened over the situation. They started meeting together to intercede for revival. They met in a barn outside their town several nights a week, interceding and praying for a reviving touch from heaven.

This went on for weeks and months, but nothing happened. One night one of the younger men stood up and said, "Fellow believers, this is futile. Could it be that we, the very ones who are most concerned for a fresh awakening from God, are the very ones who are standing in its way?" Then he quoted from the beautiful Twenty-fourth Psalm: "Who may ascend into the hill of the LORD? And who may stand in His holy place? He who has clean hands and a pure heart, Who has not lifted up his soul to falsehood, and has not sworn deceitfully. He shall receive a blessing from the LORD and righteousness from the God of his salvation" (Ps. 24:3–5).

As these words fell from the lips of the young man, the doors of heaven burst open. The convicting power of the Holy Spirit fell upon them in such majesty that they were literally struck to the floor under deep conviction of their sins. In agony before God they poured out their confession; then the graciousness of God's forgiveness flooded their souls, and the glory of the Lord filled the barn. They felt as though they were lifted up into the very presence of God.

When the men recovered from the glory of their experience, they made their way back into town. It was now the early hours of the morning. When they arrived, they saw a multitude of the townspeople gathered at the police station. They thought some tragedy had occurred. But they discovered that at the very moment the Spirit of God had gripped them in deep conviction in the barn, the all-pervasive Holy Spirit had fallen in convicting power upon a multitude of the people, revealing to them their sin and need of salvation. The people were under such conviction they didn't know what to do. So they had gathered at the police station, hoping they could find someone who would tell them how they might find God's forgiveness and salvation. Before that night was over, a vast number had come to faith in Christ.

When God's people join in earnest, prevailing prayer, God answers gloriously. Many people will come to Christ, and the church will revel in blessings and growth. Little wonder that the Bible abounds with this truth:

Though I walk in the midst of trouble, Thou wilt revive me;
Thou wilt stretch forth Thy hand against the wrath of
    my enemies,
And Thy right hand will save me.
(Ps. 138:7)

For thus says the high and exalted One
Who lives forever, whose name is Holy,
"I dwell on a high and holy place,
And also with the contrite and lowly of spirit
In order to revive the spirit of the lowly
And to revive the heart of the contrite."
(Isa. 57:15)

"He will revive us after two days;
He will raise us up on the third day
That we may live before Him."
(Hos. 6:2)

"But now for a brief moment grace has been shown from the LORD our God, to leave us an escaped remnant and to give us a peg in His holy place, that our God may enlighten our eyes and grant us a little reviving in our bondage. For we are slaves; yet in our bondage, our God has not forsaken us, but has extended lovingkindness to us in the sight of the kings of Persia, to give us reviving to raise up the house of our God, to restore its ruins, and to give us a wall in Judah and Jerusalem."
(Ezra 9:8–9)

Yet those who wait for the LORD
Will gain new strength;
They will mount up with wings like eagles,
They will run and not get tired,
They will walk and not become weary.
(Isa. 40:31)

These brief passages make it clear that God answers the fervent corporate prayers of his people.

PRAYING IN THE SPIRIT

The principle of prevailing prayer to God that brings revival blessings can be summarized in Paul's phrase, "pray at all times in the Spirit" (Eph. 6:18). The Holy Spirit serves as the "professor" in the "university of prayer." He inspires, instructs, leads, enables, and directs the God-centered prayers of God's people to God's throne room. The Holy Spirit actually prays through the submissive believer. He intercedes with "groanings too deep for words" (Rom. 8:26). All authentic, prevailing prayer emerges out of the moving of the Spirit. Become sensitive to his voice; he alone knows how to pray *unto God!*

We will be saying even more about prayer in a subsequent chapter; it stands as absolutely vital to revival and growth. A companion of prayer is Bible study for effective discipleship.

THE PLACE OF THE WORD OF GOD

In drawing close to God, it is essential that we come to grips with the Word of God. Too many church members know very little about the Bible. God's people need to be led to develop a deep thirst for the holy Scriptures. The Bible itself is filled with admonitions about this discipline. Our Lord urged believers to "search the Scriptures" (John 5:39). If we are to be true disciples of Christ, Bible study assumes a central role. One can never walk in the Spirit apart from a consistent study of the Word of God. Paul makes this clear when he says, "So then faith cometh by hearing, and hearing by the word of God" (Rom. 10:17 KJV).

A vibrant, revived faith develops from the assimilation of God's truth through the Word. The Lord Jesus himself relied on the Scriptures during his testing time in the wilderness. In the temptation narratives of Matthew and Luke, Jesus defeated Satan by his skillful use of the Word of God. The Scriptures will also do several things for us during our testing times.

The Bible helps us recognize the enemy. To identify the foe is not always easy. Satan can even appear "as an angel of light" (2 Cor. 11:14). If the devil were to come to us and say, "I'm the old serpent, and I want you to do this," few true believers would listen. But he creeps in craftily and whispers, "I am the voice of God, and here is what he wants you to do." If we are alive to the truth of God's Word, we know the Holy Spirit never leads us into any act that is contradictory to the Scriptures or that fails to glorify Jesus Christ. The Bible is a valuable tool that enables us to identify the temptations of Satan, and that holds for the church corporately.

The Bible, as seen, also instructs believers in discerning the will of God. The leadership of the Holy Spirit comes by understanding the word of Christ. We must learn by the Spirit to interpret the Bible correctly and fully. In the third temptation of Jesus, Satan attempted to lead our Lord astray by quoting the Scriptures. However, he applied it incorrectly. Our Lord turned the situation around and defeated Satan by appealing to the Word of God and interpreting and applying it properly.

Finally, the Bible inspires, strengthens, and develops our walk with Christ. Through the Scriptures, Christians learn of their identification with Christ in his death and resurrection. The more we study, the deeper these truths are impressed upon us by the Holy Spirit, and the more we learn to rest upon their trust. Faith is the victory that overcomes the world (1 John 5:4). The Bible makes us aware of the resources that are ours in Jesus Christ. Thus, we are encouraged to claim all God has said. Faith takes hold of God's promises in the Scriptures, fills life with victory, and moves us into a successful, Christlike lifestyle.

The Word of God takes a vital place in reviving discipleship. Thus, the disciplines of prayer and Bible study must become a daily habit ingrained in church members if they wish to experience God's best and bear fruit for him. This leads to the last of the disciplines, fruitfulness.

FRUITFULNESS

The "fruit of the Spirit" is defined in Galatians 5:22–23. Paul wrote, "The fruit of the Spirit is love, joy, peace, patience, kindness, goodness, faithfulness, gentleness, self-control; against such things there is no law." The fruit of a Christian centers in developing a Christlike, fruitful character. In John 15 the Lord Jesus gives a beautiful progression of fruitfulness. He says that those who abide in Him bear "fruit" (v. 2), "more fruit" (v. 2), and "much fruit" (v. 5). This progression from "fruit" to "more fruit" to "much fruit" results in a believer's hungering for holiness, crowning Christ as the sovereign Lord of life and practicing the disciplines of discipleship.

This spiritual lifestyle turns disciples into fruitful witnessing instruments in the hands of the Holy Spirit. He uses us to lead others to Jesus Christ by example and word. In this sense, the fruit of a Christian is another Christian. This is brought about by a godly life and a Spirit-led witness. Abiding in Christ as a committed disciple is essential for significant church growth. Again, let it be said when the Spirit of God falls in revival power, discipleship flourishes.

NOT AN EASY ASSIGNMENT

Discipleship is not an easy road to travel. But we do not become mature disciples by slavishly "keeping the law" any more than we are saved by the law. Discipleship progress centers in a *walk of faith*. We live by faith in our identification with Christ in life and death. Paul put it this way, "I have been crucified with Christ; and it is no longer I who live, but Christ lives in me; and the life which I now live in the flesh I live by faith in the Son of God, who loved me, and delivered Himself up for me" (Gal. 2:20). Paul expressed it more fully and completely in Romans 6:1–4: "What shall we say then? Are we to continue in sin so that grace may increase? May it never be! How shall we who died to sin still live in it? Or do you not know that all of us who have been baptized into Christ Jesus have been baptized into His death? Therefore we have been buried with Him through baptism into death, in order that as Christ was raised from the dead through the glory of the Father, so we too might walk in newness of life."

What a wonderful position is ours in Christ. In him we have died to sin and been made alive unto God. By faith we claim our position in Christ. This becomes the secret of victory over temptation and sin. This is why Jesus said, "My load is light" (Matt. 11:30). When we claim by faith our identification with Christ in death and resurrection, our Lord gives us the victory. God's grace of the Spirit enables us to bear his load. He makes it "light" so that we experience genuine delight in walking in the abiding fellowship and victory of Jesus Christ. Thus, Peter could declare that we "rejoice with joy unspeakable and full of glory" (1 Pet. 1:8 KJV).

We truly are conquerors in Christ Jesus. Nothing fills life with more meaning than the abiding fellowship of Jesus through faith— even though this means living a disciplined life in Christ. Once a relationship with him is established by grace through faith, then we have the joy of developing a dynamic fellowship with our living Lord through the sanctification process.

THE RESULTS

We enjoy many benefits of fellowship with Christ because of our position in him. We find identity—personally and corporately. The believer who walks in discipleship understands who he or she is in Christ. This translates into the entire body of Christ. As discipleship deepens, identity rises. The church as a whole comes to understand its place in the kingdom of God and begins to move and serve in this context percipitating genuine growth.

Furthermore, the disciplined disciple and church begin to set meaningful goals. When God's people know their identity in Christ and acquire an awareness of life's purpose, meaningful goals for themselves and the church can be set. Rick Warren states there are ten ways that purpose can motivate and drive a church. He lists them as follows:

1. Assimilate new members on purpose.
2. Program around your purpose.
3. Educate your people on purpose.
4. Start small groups on purpose.
5. Add staff on purpose.
6. Structure on purpose.
7. Preach on purpose.
8. Budget on purpose.
9. Calendar on purpose.
10. Evaluate on purpose.[19]

Warren's outline forms a practical, pragmatic approach to a church reaching its goals of growth. Goals are important. These goals should grow out of the believer's personal, purposeful identity with Christ in discipleship. We shall be viewing such growth principles in more depth later, but a few words on the subject of goals seems appropriate here.

GOALS

Setting church goals gives tangible direction and creates motivation. As stated earlier, every church should write a purpose statement and gather the entire life of the congregation around this purpose. When the purpose of the church is outlined clearly around biblical principles, goals can be set to achieve the purpose. Goals should have four qualities. (1) They should be challenging. Business as usual will not get the work accomplished. (2) Goals should be attainable. To set unrealistic goals actually discourages people more than it motivates them to strive for excellence. (3) Goals should be measurable. It does little good to generalize and say something like, "Let's have the greatest year in the life of the church." This really says nothing that people can get a grip on. Goals should be tangible in the sense that they can be understood and measured. (4) Goals should be scrutinized and evaluated. Perhaps a certain goal needs to be reevaluated and changed during the next planning cycle. And it must never be forgotten that the ultimate goal is to reach the world for Christ.

REACHING THE WORLD FOR THE KINGDOM

All evangelistic growth begins with a burden and concern for unbelievers—those who do not know our Lord Jesus Christ. If we take seriously what the New Testament says in this regard, we must assume a burden for the salvation of lost people. They truly are lost, cut off from God, alienated from "the commonwealth of Israel" (Eph. 2:12). Jesus said, "He who does not believe has been judged already, because he has not believed in the name of the only begotten Son of God" (John 3:18b). What is this judgment? The Book of Revelation declares, "If anyone's name was not found written in the book of life, he was thrown into the lake of fire" (Rev. 20:15). Thus, the bringing of people to faith in Jesus Christ stands as the most vital spiritual ministry a church can undertake. To fail to evangelize the unbelieving world is a sin against God and a crime against a lost world.

The tragedy of an eternity in outer darkness, where there is "weeping and gnashing of teeth" (Matt. 8:12), becomes unthinkable. This is a fact that must be faced by the church. Only the Holy Spirit can empower and lead God's people into the realization of these truths and motivate them to evangelism. May God revive us mightily to this end.

At the same time, we must admit that the church itself often seems to be "lost." With lack of proper scriptural priorities and balance, with apathy and unconcern, with laxity in moral and ethical living, with little spiritual concern for the dynamics of the Christian life, the church itself can flounder about on a turbulent sea. As James put it, a church can be "tossed by the wind" (James 1:6) and lose itself in the process. The church must be "saved" if this is its condition. The answer to this quandary is again spiritual awakening! Only God, coming in reviving power upon the church, can save it from self-destruction. But when the church becomes truly revived, its burden for the lost world is rekindled, it understands its ministry role, and it goes forward to significant outreach growth.

MOTIVATION

How can the church be motivated to address such multiple needs? Pastors and church leaders generally feel they are responsible for motivating the congregation to growth, maturity in godliness, and service. Although the Holy Spirit does use human instruments, the responsibility for motivation rests primarily on the Holy Spirit. This does not mean that we become passive in attempting to motivate people. But we must recognize that lasting motivation comes from God alone; hence the need of powerful movings of the Holy Spirit through the body of Christ.

Too often we dream up new ideas, plans, and schemes, thinking they will stimulate our people into service. And they may work for a short time. But they soon lose their attractiveness, and we have to come up with something new. Finally, a backlash develops so that people cannot be motivated by anything. We must learn to rely completely on the motivating work of the Holy Spirit. This means much prayer and searching the Scriptures. It certainly means finding his leadership in our planning. So we are back to the spiritual disciplines again. Ministry grows when God's people abide in Christ and feel comfortable and confident with the Holy Spirit's guiding and empowering the body. Then they begin to serve Christ on the basis of their spiritual gifts. This brings us to the principle of the lay-centered ministry.

THE LAY-CENTERED MINISTRY

If we believe that God's Spirit empowers and gives gifts to *all* Christians, we can launch out on this principle to see all of God's people assuming their respective responsibilities. The priesthood of all believers is founded on this principle. We all have been gifted by the Holy Spirit. As pointed out earlier, every believer has a "spiritual gift" with which to serve Christ (1 Cor. 12). Such an approach to Christian service is practical. It makes people feel inadequate for the task, inspiring responsibility in Christ's servants. Every believer can do what God wills in ministry. We can expect God's power and blessings and leadership to fall on us when we exercise our ministry gifts. This quality of service can bring glory to Jesus Christ. The laypeople must be liberated to discover and exercise their gifts.

A HOLISTIC DISCIPLESHIP MINISTRY

God's wants his people to serve him on a need-motivated basis. The Lord Jesus Christ presents the perfect example; he stepped into people's lives right where they hurt. If they were hungry, he fed them. If they were sick, he healed them. If they needed comfort and cheer, he touched them with his positive spirit. If they languished in sin and guilt, he met this need in forgiveness and salvation. Our Lord did not "cubbyhole" needs. He saw people in their plight and stepped in to meet their needs. There has never been a great spiritual awakening where this type of ministry has not surfaced.

In the revival that surrounded the ministry of Charles Haddon Spurgeon, more than twenty ministries grew out of his Metropolitan Tabernacle work. Under the leadership of the reviving Holy Spirit, Spurgeon founded old people's homes, educational ministries, orphanages—even unwed mother's homes, which was a radical innovation in Victorian England. During the Second Great Awakening in America, more than six hundred Christian colleges were established. Other great results of this movement were the founding of hospitals, orphanages, and the moral transformation of the Western frontier. When real revival comes, the church begins to minister. A holistic ministry always surfaces in spiritual awakening. This impacts the community, and the church experiences significant growth.

CONCLUSION

When revival bursts on the scene, four marvelous fallouts occur: (1) discipleship deepens, (2) ministry multiplies, (3) the church evangelizes with zeal and makes new disciples, and (4) real growth takes place. Do we want to see God ripen the field and bring growth to the church? Then we must take seriously the basic premise of this book. Growth comes when spiritual awakening occurs and when we use good methods as faithful disciples of Jesus Christ. We should seek these spiritual discipleship qualities. They are foundational to building great churches. Then we can move out in Spirit-led programs that will turn entire communities to Jesus Christ.

TEN QUESTIONS FOR STUDY

1. Who were the Puritan-Pietists?
2. Was the Puritan-Pietist movement positive and valid? Why?
3. What place does emotion have in a real revival, and what are its dangers?
4. What is the meaning of *discipleship?*
5. How does a hunger for holiness develop in a believer's life?
6. Why is prayer so central to the entire Christian experience?
7. What does it mean to pray "unto God" and how does prayer relate to discipleship?
8. How does the Bible figure in discipleship?
9. How does one discipline oneself to become a disciple?
10. What has all this to do with church growth?

CHAPTER 6

EVANGELISM IN SPIRITUAL AWAKENING AND CHURCH GROWTH

To title a chapter "Evangelism and Spiritual Awakening in Church Growth" sounds almost redundant. Recall that Donald McGavran searched for a word to replace *evangelism* because of the "baggage" the term had acquired, and he came up with "church growth." For McGavran, evangelism and church growth were synonymous. But the phrase "church growth" means more than evangelization today. Churches grow in spirituality and in social ministries as well as in numbers.

But if we aspire to see a church grow, with its ultimate goal being kingdom extension, evangelization becomes essential. We often see churches growing primarily by the transferring of membership from one congregation or denomination to another. But if the Kingdom itself is to grow, along with local churches as well, evangelization is a mandatory ministry, and effective evangelism always becomes the fruit of true spiritual awakening. An in-depth look at the issue is thus in order. We begin by examining a misconception concerning the enterprise of evangelization.

A MISCONCEPTION

Some people argue that outreach growth is predicated primarily on sociological factors, such as church buildings being properly located, advertising, programs, and so forth. They point to the need to be in a booming urban area into which large numbers of people and families are moving, to have our buildings in high-visibility spots with easy access. They believe these factors are essential ingredients for church growth.

Such factors certainly have their place. A cursory look at the business world attests to this reality. For example, where do you see the "golden arches" of McDonalds? They can always be found on busy thoroughfares or major intersections with good accessibility and high visibility. These principles to some extent do serve as aids to the growth of individual churches, but they do not provide the final answer to extensive evangelistic outreach. Many churches have excellent locations, but they find themselves stagnated as far as evangelistic growth is concerned. On the other hand, some churches have poor access and visibility, but they explode with growth. An excellent illustration comes from rural Kentucky.

Several years ago, a personal friend, Dr. Robert Jackson, served as pastor of a typical First Baptist Church in a southern state. He carried on a traditional ministry and experienced a measure of God's blessings. As a young man, he seemed to be moving toward a good ministry when he suffered a serious heart attack. His ministry was put on hold for a long period. After recovering a measure of health, he became the pastor of a small rural church in central Kentucky. It seemed an unlikely spot to carry on a great ministry for a pastor who held a Ph.D. degree.

During his illness, this man of God had a deep and enriching spiritual experience. God's Spirit awakened and revived him in a profound fashion. As his strength allowed, he threw himself into the work of the little country congregation. The church building was bordered by a state road on one side and empty fields on the other. Across the highway was a little spot of land, but it was cut off by a creek. This limitation did not deter this pastor or the Lord. God began to move in a marvelous fashion. It can only be described as real revival coming to that little rural church. It began to be evident to those who lived in the area that something unusual was taking place in that rather traditional country congregation.

People began to come in increasing numbers. As they came, many found Christ as their Savior. The ministry of this church today can only be described as phenomenal. They have burst the seams of their structures; their impact on the area has been revolutionary. A multitude has come to new commitment to Christ. And because God instilled in this congregation a kingdom vision—which the Holy Spirit always does when he revives his people—they began to cast an eye on the whole world and its needs.

In the providence of God, Romania got on their heart. Through much prayer and work, ministry teams began to travel to that former communist country. Dr. Jackson's rural church started planting new congregations in Romania. To date, there have been some two dozen churches established in Romania from that little country church in central Kentucky—although the Kentucky church is not little in numbers or spirit anymore.

When true spiritual awakening grips a people, evangelism and a worldwide vision come alive with a fervency unprecedented in the normal run of church life. Perhaps the word *normal* is a misnomer for describing the average church. Many congregations may be "normal" from our contemporary cultural perspective. But in the New Testament era, evangelistic fervency with a worldwide commitment vibrated through the people of God. This was the norm. Actually, a revival is no more—or no less—than a return to normal New Testament Christianity.

EVANGELISM AND THE *MISSIO DEI*

It has become clear that evangelism assumes a vital, central role in the mission of God, the *misseo dei*. But what constitutes God's total mission? What is God doing in this world through his church? What is the ultimate goal? This must become the guiding motivation of any congregation if it aspires to fulfill its mission and to experience the blessings of our Lord. When we pray "Thy kingdom come," we cannot escape the conclusion that God's mission becomes the church's mission. The *missio dei* can be expressed in a few words: God is at work in the world to shape his *entire universe* into the very image of Jesus Christ. The apostle Paul wrote to the Romans, "That the creation itself also will be set free from its slavery to corruption into the freedom of the glory of the children of God. For we know that the whole creation groans and suffers the pains of childbirth together until now. And not only this, but also we ourselves, having the first fruits of the Spirit, even we ourselves groan within ourselves, waiting eagerly for our adoption as sons, the redemption of our body" (Rom. 8:21–23).

Paul recognized this principle clearly when he said to the Galatians, "My children, with whom I am again in labor until *Christ is formed in you*" (Gal. 4:19, author's italics). God is "forming" Christ in the church and ultimately in all creation. That mission applies to the individual and to the entire church alike. Actually, God is working in the whole created order to fashion it into the image of his Son.[1] The day will come, as the Bible describes it, when "the kingdom of the world has become the kingdom of our Lord, and of His Christ; and He will reign forever and ever" (Rev. 11:15b).

What a glorious day that will be when Christ returns, and all sin, evil, corruption, and Satan himself will be expelled. Christ will reign and all wrongs will be put right. In the meantime, we must evangelize and prepare multitudes for that great day. Oswald J. Smith, the late great pastor of the People's Church of Toronto, Canada, wrote some years ago:

When the Lord Jesus Christ left this world, 1,900 years ago, He gave His disciples just one thing to do. He spoke in effect as follows: I am leaving you now. I will be gone a long time, but one of these days I will return. Now, while I am absent there is just one thing I want you to do. I want you to take this Gospel of mine and give it to the entire world. See that every tribe, people, tongue and nation hears it. Do you understand? Then, when you have done it, I will be back, but not before. With these words He left them and they went to work. During the first generation they did a fine job. They succeeded in preaching His Gospel to most of the then known world.[2]

To prepare the world for Christ's divine hour is God's mission. He involves his church in this task. We must come to an understanding of evangelism's role in the overall *missio dei*.

THE ROLE

Our Lord Jesus Christ placed the primacy of evangelism center stage in the mission of God when he said, "The Son of Man has come to seek and to save that which was lost" (Luke 19:10). The essential mission of our Lord—his number one priority as the Good Shepherd—was to find the one lost sheep and bring it into his fold. This is why Jesus died and rose again. He came to save his lost sheep—you and me. Since this is the heart of our Lord's ministry, it surely must be true of his church in its ministry. If the essence of the Christ event moved to evangelistic ends, how can the church be lackadaisical in its evangelistic commitment? An honest, objective look at the New Testament brings us to the conclusion that evangelism is the foundation stone for all Christian ministries. It rests right at the core of the *missio dei;* it must therefore rest at the core of the church's life. The poet expressed it well:

Give us a watchword for the hour,
A thrilling word, a word of power;
A battle-cry, a flaming breath
That calls to conquest or to death;
A word to rouse the church from rest,
To heed her Master's high behest,
The call is given: Ye hosts arise,
Our watchword is Evangelize!

The glad evangel now proclaim
Through all the earth in Jesus' name;
This word is ringing through the skies,

Evangelize! Evangelize!
To dying men, a fallen race,
Make known the gift of gospel grace;
The world that now in darkness lies,
Evangelize! Evangelize![3]

Considerable confusion reigns in church life today about the nature of evangelism. This issue demands a look.

THE MEANING OF EVANGELISM

There have been several definitions given for *evangelism*. Here are some sample definitions:

To evangelize is so to present Christ Jesus in the power of the Holy Spirit that men shall come to put their trust in God through Him, to accept Him as their Savior, and serve Him as their King in the fellowship of His church.

—Archbishop of Canterbury's Committee on Evangelism

Evangelism is going to the people outside. It is the proclamation of the good news of God in Jesus Christ to "Them that are without" . . . it is the sheer work of the herald . . . He blows the trumpet and demands to be heard.

—W. E. Sangster, Methodist pastor of London

Evangelism is the task of reaching outside the church to bring people to faith in Christ and membership in His church.

—George Sweazy, Princeton Seminary professor

Evangelism is one beggar telling another beggar where to find bread.

—D. T. Niles, missiologist of Sri Lanka

Evangelism is a concerted, self-conscious effort to confront the unbeliever with the truth about and the claims of Christ with a view to challenging and leading that unbeliever into repentance toward God and faith in our Lord Jesus Christ and thus into the fellowship of His church that spiritual growth may occur.

—Lewis A. Drummond, professor of evangelism

What do these definitions mean? What are the implications? Perhaps it would be wise to outline initially what biblical evangelism is not.

First, evangelism cannot claim to be *everything* the church does. This defines the enterprise far too broadly. Such an approach may even be deceptive in that it can take the edge off pointed, intentional evangelism. The church engages in many ministries. As various needs arise, the church should meet those needs in Christ's name. Every ministry in which the church engages may contribute in some indirect way to evangelization, but evangelism must not be seen as a generic term that covers the entire life of the church.

Second, evangelism is far more than the minister standing in the pulpit on Sunday morning "preaching the gospel." This makes the enterprise far too narrow. To understand evangelism from this restricted perspective also has some subtle dangers. Not only is it too narrow, but it tends to excuse the congregation as a whole from engaging in the church's evangelistic task. The Great Commission to make disciples of all nations is incumbent upon all believers.

Third, evangelism is not just "living a good life," with the hope that someone will observe and be drawn to Christ. This author on one occasion was sharing in a seminar on evangelization. Someone in the group said, "Well, I do not believe that you should do any more than just live a good testimony before people, and that will bring them to Christ." Everyone who names the name of Christ should live an exemplary life that points people to the Lord, but evangelism involves more than this. It means *declaring* the gospel as well as living it.

Fourth, evangelism is not proselytizing. To enlist people for the institution's sake, just to fill pews and make our records look good, is a far cry from fulfilling the *missio dei*. How easy it is to slip into the syndrome of enlisting people for our own sake. But this error has been emphasized sufficiently.

Finally, evangelism must not be equated with merely creating "decisions" and forcing people into our ecclesiastical mold. This can be very superficial and even bring about decisions that are not salvific. An evangelism without integrity can deceive people, delude the church, and spell ultimate, final tragedy for people. Our Lord said, "Not everyone who says to Me, 'Lord, Lord,' will enter the kingdom of heaven; but he who does the will of My Father who is in heaven. Many will say to Me on that day, 'Lord, Lord, did we not prophesy in Your name, and in Your name cast out demons, and in Your name perform many miracles?' And then I will declare to them, 'I never knew you; DEPART FROM ME, YOU WHO PRACTICE LAWLESSNESS'" (Matt. 7:21–23). God save us from precipitating superficial decisions and deceiving people.

WHAT EVANGELISM IS

Now to a more positive approach. What is evangelism of integrity from the biblical perspective?

The first principle to establish is that all biblical evangelism must stem from a proper motive. The New Testament presents three motivations as the rationale and reason for doing evangelism. The first is that evangelism comes as a command of our Lord: "Thus it is written, that the Christ should suffer and rise again from the dead the third day; and that repentance for forgiveness of sins should be proclaimed in His name to all the nations, beginning from Jerusalem. You are witnesses of these things" (Luke 24:46–48).

We must confess that we do not always abide on a high spiritual level. But whether we find ourselves on a spiritual mountaintop, experiencing a high motivation to share Christ, or in a valley of struggle, our Lord *commands* us to share the gospel. Times and circumstances arise when we must discipline ourselves and do what God commands, whether we feel like it or not. Thus, the Scripture presents the injunction for all God's people, in all situations, in all of life, "in season and out of season" (2 Tim. 4:2), to help others to faith in Christ.

Another motive the Bible lifts up as a higher goal is the motive of love. Paul said in 2 Corinthians 5:14, "The love of Christ controls us, having concluded this, that one died for all, therefore all died." Love for people and their dire need of salvation should move us to lead them to Jesus Christ. When we realize they are lost, love spurs us on to help them find the Savior.

The final motive is extolling the glory of God. Paul said, "Whether, then, you eat or drink or whatever you do, do all to the glory of God" (1 Cor. 10:31). This becomes the highest motivation for evangelism. When we seek God's glory alone in evangelism, as well as in all of life, our Lord will honor our efforts.

Another positive note about evangelism is that biblical evangelism confronts people as people. It sees them as individuals and people groups who desperately need the Lord Jesus Christ. Of course, the Savior himself stands as the high example. Matthew tells us in his Gospel: "Seeing the multitudes, He [Jesus] felt compassion for them, because they were distressed and downcast like sheep without a shepherd" (9:36). We must never see people as mere objects but as precious souls for whom Christ died.

Furthermore, biblical evangelism presents the full gospel of Christ in every way possible. The Book of Acts makes this clear. The early disciples went to people in prison, addressed the synagogues, shared in the message by the riverside. In a word, they witnessed in the normal traffic pattern of life. They addressed people with the gospel wherever they encountered them. This implies that evangelization is always to some extent confrontational; we go to people with a message. Paul said to the Ephesian church leaders that he constantly engaged in "solemnly testifying to both Jews and Greeks of repentance toward God and faith in our Lord Jesus Christ" (Acts 20:21).

Biblical evangelization means confronting people and leading them to a genuine decision of repentance toward God and faith in our Lord Jesus Christ. And this is inevitably confrontational. While we should confront people in love and in a gracious manner, they must be addressed with the truth. And of course, evangelism according to Christ enlists people into the Christian community so that the discipleship process may be nurtured and developed.

All of this implies that the person who witnesses to others must have an understanding of the gospel. We cannot evangelize if we have a faulty grasp of the Good News. What constitutes the message that Paul called "the power of God for salvation" (Rom. 1:16)? What did the apostle mean when he wrote to the Corinthians that the proclamation of Christ (*kerygma*) brings people to faith in the Lord Jesus (1 Cor. 1:21)?

THE CONTENT OF EVANGELISTIC PROCLAMATION

Although one never appreciates the type of sharing that grows out of a bigoted and narrow dogmatism, there must be no "uncertain sound" from the witness in sharing the Good News. As theologian Douglas Webster reminds us:

A mood of uncertainty about the heart of the Gospel, the Lord of the Church, and the Savior of the world, is unworthy of Christians and bodes ill for the future of missions if it is allowed to be encouraged or persists. Describing the first mission to Thessalonica, St. Paul wrote: "When we brought you the gospel, we brought it not in mere words but in the power of the Holy Spirit, and with strong conviction, as you know well" (1 Thess. 1:5 NEB). Christian, even theological, humility is not synonymous with vagueness.[4]

What then is our message?

C. H. DODD'S APPROACH TO THE *KERYGMA*

C. H. Dodd, New Testament scholar, penned a classic small volume entitled *The Apostolic Preaching and Its Development*. This book aroused much interest in the idea conveyed by the New Testament Greek word *kerygma*, i.e., the "proclamation." In his work Dodd argued for a distinction between *kerygma* and another New Testament word, *didache*, or teaching. *Didaskein* means the ethical and moral instructions on the Christian life and certain aspects of theology. Dodd contended that *didaskein* is quite different from *kerygma*. *Kerygma* means the "public proclamation of Christianity to the non-Christian world."[5] In the first century, it was by *kerygma* that the church evangelized. As Paul said in 1 Corinthians 1:21: "For since in the wisdom of God the world through its wisdom did not come to know God, God was well-pleased through the foolishness of the message preached (*kerygma*) to save those who believe."

Dodd contended that the basic idea contained in the term *kerygma* is so close to that conveyed by the word *evangelion* (the "gospel," Rom. 1:16) that for all practical purposes the two terms can be used synonymously.[6] Thus he deduced: "For the early church, then to preach the Gospel was by no means the same thing as to deliver moral instruction or exhortation. While the church was concerned to hand on the teaching of the Lord, it was not by this that it made converts. It was by *kerygma*, says Paul, not by *didache*, that it pleased God to save men."[7]

So again we must ask, "What is this primary *kerygma*—the essence of the proclamation to win people to Jesus Christ?" In other words, what is the gospel of Christ? Considering the preaching of Peter and others in early Acts, in the Jerusalem area, Dodd outlined six basic elements in their *kerygma*.

1. The age of fulfillment has dawned. The messianic age has arrived (Acts 2:16 ff).

2. This new age has come through the ministry, death, and resurrection of Jesus Christ, and a brief account of this is always given. The concepts of the Davidic descent, the Lord's ministry, his vicarious death, and his glorious resurrection are proclaimed. Moreover, these truths are presented in the context of scriptural prophecy fulfilled as determined by the foreknowledge of God.

3. By virtue of the resurrection, our Lord has been elevated to the right hand of God as messianic head of the "new Israel" (Acts 2:33–36).

4. The Holy Spirit came as the sign of Christ's present power and glory (Acts 2:33).

5. The messianic age will reach its consummation in the return of Christ (Acts 3:21).

6. The *kerygma* in Acts always closes with an appeal for repentance, the offer of forgiveness, the gift of the Holy Spirit, and the assurance of salvation in the life of the "age to come" (Acts 2:38–39).

Dodd then summarized, "We may take it that this is what the author of Acts meant by 'preaching the kingdom of God.'"[8]

Paul preached to Gentiles, and in the context of the Roman world he declared:

• The prophecies are fulfilled and the new age is inaugurated by the coming of Christ.

• He was born of the seed of David.

• He died according to the Scriptures, to deliver us out of the present evil age.

• He was buried.

• He rose on the third day according to the Scriptures.

• He is exalted at the right hand of God, as Son of God and Lord of quick and dead.

• He will come again as Judge and Savior of men.[9]

Dodd says that perhaps the evangelistic preaching of Paul contained more than the above elements. But preaching must have the above elements if it is to be called evangelistic proclamation.

Something of a contrast exists between the Pauline proclamation and the Jerusalem *kerygma*. Dodd points out three aspects of the contrast. (1) In early Acts Jesus is rarely called the "Son of God," as was true later of Paul. The prophecies of Isaiah, by and large, account for the messianic terminology he used. Yet the idea of Jesus as Son of God is deeply embodied in the Synoptic Gospels. (2) Peter's Jerusalem *kerygma* as over against Paul's Gentile preaching says little about Christ dying *for our sins*. As Dodd puts it, "The result of the life, death, and resurrection of Christ is the forgiveness of sins, but the forgiveness is not specifically connected with his death."[10] But it must be understood that Paul had more time to work out a concept of the atonement where early Acts did not; hence, Paul connected Christ's death with the Old Testament sacrifices as securing forgiveness. (3) The Jerusalem *kerygma* does not emphasize that the ascended Lord intercedes for us, as did Paul. As for the rest of the points in Peter and Paul's gospels, they are the same. And where the contrast does exist, the reason centers in the fact that Paul was the Apostle to the Gentiles, Peter the Apostle to the Jews. They understood the need of culturalizing the gospel—a strategic move and the rationale for doing so today.

MICHAEL GREEN AND THE *KERYGMA*

Evaluations of C. H. Dodd's approach to the gospel have naturally arisen. For example, Michael Green feels that Dodd made the *kerygma* too fixed. He argues that "the probabilities of the situation would militate against undue fixity in the presentation of the message."[11] What should be grasped, Green contends, is that the background and understanding of the listeners helped determine what aspect of the truth of Christ should be preached. Still, Green grants, "There was a basic homogeneity in what was preached."

What then makes up this "basic homogeneity" according to New Testament scholar Michael Green? He believes we will be wise in elucidating only three basic points as essential to the word that the first-century church proclaimed. (1) The early church preached a person. Their message was unapologetically Christocentric. The gospel message is about Jesus Christ, his life and public ministry climaxing in his death and glorious resurrection. (2) The early church proclaimed a gift; the gift of forgiveness, the Holy Spirit, adoption, and reconciliation. God's quality of grace made "no people" the "people of God." In the area of the gift, the emphasis fell on the gift of forgiveness and the gift of the Holy Spirit. (3) The first-century proclaimers expected a response. The church asked people to decide then and there for or against Christ. With faith in the power of the gospel, they anticipated positive results. These early preachers urged people to come to Christ. The respondents must do three things in the light of the message of salvation.

1. They must first repent toward God.
2. They must exercise faith in Christ—a continuing life of faith. Of course, true faith is inseparable from repentance.
3. The apostles preached baptism as the seal on God's offer of forgiveness. The visible essence of repentance centered in this act.

From this perspective, Green gives his understanding of the essential *kerygma*. And he seems correct, at least to a degree, in his evaluation of Dodd's more inflexible approach. A witness must be sensitive to the hearer's background, culture, and understanding. Yet the full gospel must be communicated. We cannot rely on clichés, slogans, and simple summaries. This approach can bring about shallow if not superficial decisions. As John Stott has said:

When we contrast much contemporary evangelism with Paul's, its shallowness is immediately shown up. Our evangelism tends to be too ecclesiastical (inviting people to church), whereas Paul also took the gospel out into the secular world; too emotional (appeals for decision without an adequate basis of understanding), whereas Paul taught, reasoned and tried to persuade; and too superficial (making brief encounters and expecting quick results), whereas Paul stayed in Corinth and Ephesus for five years, faithfully sowing gospel seed and in due time reaping a harvest.[12]

Furthermore, an important place for apologetics exists in gospel proclamation. Especially is this true today. With the passing of "modernity"—and as we enter into the "postmodern" era with its manifestations in New Age concepts and its emphases on spirituality but loss of absolutes—we must be able to break down false walls so the gospel will receive a hearing. Paul did this in his Athenian address to the philosophical sophisticates at the Athenian Areopagus (Acts 17:16–34). A lengthy quote from John Stott strikes at the heart of the issue:

Paul's reaction to the city's idolatry was not negative only (horror and dismay) but also positive and constructive (witness). He did not merely throw up his hands in despair, or weep helplessly, or curse and swear at the Athenians. No, he shared with them the good news of Jesus. He sought by the proclamation of the gospel to prevail on them to turn from their idols to the living God and so to give to him and to his Son the glory due to their name. The stirrings of his spirit with righteous indignation opened his mouth in testimony. We observe the three groups with whom Luke tells us he spoke. First, following his usual practice, he went to the synagogue on the sabbath and "reasoned" there with both Jews and God-fearers. As in Thessalonica, so in Athens, he will have delineated the Christ of Scripture, proclaimed the Jesus of history, and identified the two as the heaven-sent Savior of sinners. Secondly, he went into the *agora*, which has now been completely excavated and restored, and which did duty as both marketplace and center of public life, and argued there with "casual passers-by" (NEB), not now on the sabbath but *day by day*. He seems deliberately to have adopted the famous Socratic method of dialogue, involving questions and answers; he was, in fact, a kind of Christian Socrates, although with a better gospel than Socrates ever knew.

Thirdly, Epicurean and Stoic philosophers began to dispute with him, and he with them. These were contemporary but rival systems. The Epicureans, or "philosophers of the garden," founded by Epicurus (died 270 B.C.), considered the gods to be so remote as to take no interest in, and have no influence on, human affairs. The world was due to chance, a random concourse of atoms, and there would be no survival of death, and no judgement. So human beings should pursue pleasure, especially the serene enjoyment of a life detached from pain, passion and fear. The Stoics, however, or "philosophers of the porch" (the *stoa* or painted colonnade next to the

agora where they taught), founded by Zeno (died 265 B.C),
acknowledged the supreme god but in a pantheistic way, confusing him with the "world soul." The world was determined
by fate, and human beings must pursue their duty, resigning
themselves to live in harmony with nature and reason, however painful this might be, and develop their own self-
sufficiency. To oversimplify, it was characteristic of Epicureans
to emphasize chance, escape and the enjoyment of pleasure,
and of the Stoics to emphasize fatalism, submission and the
endurance of pain. In Paul's later speech to the Areopagus we
hear echoes of the encounter between the gospel and these
philosophies, as he refers to the caring activity of a personal
Creator, the dignity of human beings as his "offspring," the
certainty of judgement and the call to repentance.

One cannot help admiring Paul's ability to speak with
equal facility to religious people in the synagogue, to casual
passers-by in the city square, and to highly sophisticated
philosophers both in the *agora* and when they met in Council.
Today the nearest equivalent to the synagogue is the church,
the place where religious people gather. There is still an important place for sharing the gospel with church-goers, God-
fearing people on the fringe of the church, who may attend
services only occasionally. The equivalent of the *agora* will vary
in different parts of the world. It may be a park, city square or
street corner, a shopping mall or marketplace, a "pub," neighborhood bar, café, discotheque or student cafeteria, wherever
people meet when they are at leisure. There is a need for gifted
evangelists who can make friends and gossip the gospel in such
informal settings as these. As for the Areopagus, it has no pre-
cise equivalent in the contemporary world. Perhaps the nearest
is the university, where many of the country's intelligentsia are
to be found. Neither church evangelism nor street evangelism
would be appropriate for them. Instead, we should develop
home evangelism in which there is free discussion, "Agnostics

Anonymous" groups in which no holds are barred, and lecture evangelism, which contains a strong apologetic content. There is an urgent need for more Christian thinkers who will dedicate their minds to Christ, not only as lecturers, but also as authors, journalists dramatists and broadcasters, as television script-writers, producers and personalities, and as artists and actors who use a variety of art forms in which to communicate the gospel. All these can do battle with contemporary non-Christian philosophies and ideologies in a way which resonates with thoughtful, modern men and women, and so at least gain a hearing for the gospel by the reasonableness of its presentation. Christ calls human beings to humble, but not to stifle, their intellect.[13]

Good advice from Stott—it gives us a lesson to learn.

LESSONS TO LEARN

Now what can we assimilate from these and other varied approaches to the *kerygma?* Three lessons seem vital. (1) As Stott points out, we must take the gospel everywhere—into the marketplace, into intellectual circles, into the church and around the world. The message is to be proclaimed regardless of obstacles. This means developing a good apologetic. (2) We must be certain we are proclaiming the gospel in person-to-person terms. There is a gracious confrontational element in evangelism. The gospel has content—biblical content—and it addresses people where they live. Certain realities must be clearly understood and declared in the presentation of the truth. This engagement centers in the person and work of Jesus Christ. (3) Our evangelistic communication must contain the essential and full *kerygma,* and we are to expect God's blessings upon our sharing. A classic biblical case can be seen in Peter's sermon on the day of Pentecost. The apostle declared:

> Men of Israel, listen to these words: Jesus the Nazarene, a
> man attested to you by God with miracles and wonders and

signs which God performed through Him in your midst, just as you yourselves know—this Man, delivered up by the predetermined plan and foreknowledge of God, you nailed to a cross by the hands of godless men and put Him to death. And God raised Him up again, putting an end to the agony of death, since it was impossible for Him to be held in its power. . . . Now when they heard this, they were pierced to the heart, and said to Peter and the rest of the apostles, "Brethren, what shall we do?" And Peter said to them, "Repent, and let each of you be baptized in the name of Jesus Christ for the forgiveness of your sins; and you shall receive the gift of the Holy Spirit." (Acts 2:22–24, 37–38)

Mere appeals to the imagination or emotions fall short of what the New Testament understands by evangelism. "We preach Christ" (1 Cor. 1:23); this must be our theme. Anyone who aspires to share the gospel must be very careful to use the essential content of the full *kerygma* and to speak in such a way that the gospel makes sense to people where they are in their cultural setting. And God expects us to trust him for positive results.

Perhaps the evangelistic enterprise can be summed up in what is implied by the word *overflow*. When God's Holy Spirit comes upon his people and they are filled with the Spirit overflowing with the grace and glory of God, evangelism in the biblical sense naturally follows. And evangelism becomes the role of the entire church. God expects all his people to serve as witnesses for Jesus Christ. But many Christians do not know how to engage in personal witnessing. Can this impediment be overcome?

AN OBSTACLE TO OVERCOME

The perfect example of effective sharing and breaking down barriers can be found in the life and ministry of our Lord Jesus Christ. He can teach us to be overcomers. Christ empowers his servants to emulate him in all things—especially sharing his truths. Ten salient and simple points emerge from the ministry of Jesus in regard to sharing with others. They become something of a pattern for evangelism from the pulpit or the pew, from the front door of the church out into the world. These ten points can teach us how to be effective, bold witnesses:

1. Jesus gave himself unreservedly. He shared his very personhood on behalf of the lost. He did this in a fashion we cannot perfectly reproduce. Yet, we must emulate the principle if we aspire to be effective "evangelists."

2. Christ confronted people with the central issues of life. He never let himself be sidetracked by theological fads or secondary issues. He held to the main point. His conversation with the Samaritan woman demonstrates this principle (John 4:5–30). Jesus always dealt with the great truths of the faith and with a marvelous simplicity. "The common people heard him gladly" (Mark 12:37 KJV). To overshoot people intellectually or culturally is to fail at following Christ's example.

3. Our Lord never compromised the demanding claims of the gospel just to win followers. He always presented his absolute lordship and the full cost of discipleship. He refused to cut corners to gain anyone. The classic illustration of this is his confrontation with the rich young ruler. In Dietrich Bonhoeffer's words, Jesus never declared "cheap grace."

4. At the same time, Christ had profound respect for people. He never rode roughshod over anyone. He was always patient, displayed understanding, exhibited a loving attitude. He refused to make anyone less of a person, even in his occasional scathing denunciations.

5. Jesus asked men and women to decide for or against him then and there. He challenged Simon and Andrew, James and John to choose immediately between their nets or following him (Mark 1:16–20). There is a time for people to wait and consider the cost (Luke 14:28–32), but there is also a time to call for decision.

6. It seems evident in the Gospels that our Lord had a definite strategy in his mission. For example, "He was journeying with

his face toward Jerusalem" (Luke 9:53). Jesus knew his role and where he was going. In modern terms, he had a program to fulfill his purpose.

7. The Lord never attempted to do all the work himself. He taught, encouraged, nurtured, and commissioned his disciples. This principle in Paul is found in 2 Timothy 2:2: "The things which you have heard from me in the presence of many witnesses, these entrust to faithful men, who will be able to teach others also."

8. Above all, Jesus showed compassion. He realized that people wandered about as sheep without a shepherd. In this context he ministered, always displaying the "spirit of the towel and basin"—that of a servant. He said, "The Son of Man did not come to be served, but to serve" (Matt. 20:28).

9. Christ ministered to the whole person. Physical, mental, and spiritual needs were met quite indiscriminately. When needs arose, he met them.

10. Our Lord understood that even for him, prayer was the one indispensable exercise for effective sharing. Thus our Lord ministered his Good News and people responded.

What about the church as a corporate entity? How is the church as the body of Christ to evangelize? A look at the day of Pentecost gives insight and a model for local church evangelism. Much more than evangelistic principles is implied by Pentecost; this day opened a great epoch for the infant church. Still, much can be learned about the church's evangelistic mission by the events of the day.

THE DAY OF PENTECOST

Pentecost declares clearly that the age of the Spirit has dawned. Our Lord did not withdraw from salvation history with his glorious ascension. He now works as profoundly as in the days of his flesh. He sent his Spirit to continue his ministry in and through his believers. All effective mission, therefore, unfolds in the context of a Spirit-led, inspired, and energized service.

Pentecost also shows that before anything significant happens in the unbelieving community, something of real significance must happen to the church. The city of Jerusalem took little note of the twelve followers of the Nazarene gathered for ten days in their upper room. But when the disciples received the Spirit's fullness, "the multitude came together" (Acts 2:6) and they were "bewildered" (v. 6), "amazed" (v. 7), and "perplexed" (v. 12) until they finally gave up trying to discover a rationale for the phenomenon and asked, "What does this mean?" (v. 12). It was then—and not until then—that Peter could stand up and say, "This is that!" (v. 16 KJV) and present Christ.

A dynamic situation such as this always sets the atmosphere for effective evangelism. People in the outside world becomes so perplexed by the wonder of what God is doing through his church that they begin asking questions. In this setting, the gospel can be communicated effectively. We all pray for such a move of God's Spirit upon his church. For the first-century believers, this brought revival in its most sublime manifestation.

On the day of Pentecost, the revived believers declared Christ powerfully. This always happens during spiritual awakening days. The disciples had only one message. This does not mean the New Testament church does not minister in many different ways. It surely does not mean they did not confront people in their own life situation and approach them with the Good News in accordance with their life setting. Stephen addressed the biblically oriented Sanhedrin. Peter appealed to the God-fearing Gentile Cornelius. Paul preached to the philosophical intellectuals of Athens. They approached these different people with their different references of thought but always presented Christ in his fullness as the answer to their basic needs.

The evangelistic thrust of the church must go worldwide—to all peoples—because all people apart from Christ are lost (Acts 4:12). Globalization is central to the furtherance of God's mission in the world and the establishing of the kingdom. Either the church evangelizes or it dies. As someone has put it: "God has no grandchildren." We either evangelize our present generation, or the church will come to an end.

The church will never rise to this incredible challenge unless God moves upon his people. Only then will it fulfill its kingdom mission. The church must thrust itself into the world empowered by the Holy Spirit, employing the best church growth methods available in order to bring Christ to the multitudes. This raises another issue: How does the church go about this task?

HOW THE CHURCH EVANGELIZES

When Jesus said, "You shall be My witnesses" (Acts 1:8), he meant the corporate church as well as the persons in the church. Church growth methodologies based on biblical principles play their role. Let's look into the ministry of Paul to see the principles that guided him in his church-centered ministry. The Book of Acts presents several methodological principles. They are as relevant to our contemporary scene as Paul found them in his day.

PAUL'S CHURCH GROWTH METHODS

The apostle Paul used the principle of "target groups." Paul knew to whom God had sent him, and he devised ways to get to them. He was a wise spiritual sociologist. His philosophy revolved around the idea, "To the Jew first and also to the Greek" (Rom. 1:16). Almost invariably Paul went first to the synagogue. This approach grew out of his deep theological commitment, but it also gave him a foothold to get to the Gentile world to whom he had been called. The strategy was simple: The apostle began where he could find a group with some measure of receptivity to spiritual truths. He used the strategy, to use Donald McGavran's words, of targeting "receptive areas." The Jews, though many of them rejected Jesus as their Messiah, still had an openness to spiritual matters. To start where people have something of a reception to the spiritual message is a wise strategy. One can then move from there to target other people groups.

Pick your goal and begin where you can—this was Paul's approach. Our "targets" will vary from culture to culture, from generation to generation, and even from church to church in any given culture. We need to set our sight on our target groups and find a way to gain an inroad and hearing. The all-wise Spirit of God will lead his people into the areas where they will find a response.

Another significant methodology of the apostle Paul was his concentration on large urban areas. He had a strategic rationale for this approach. Paul knew the largest mass of people can be found in cities. Urban centers also form a strategic base from which the gospel can spread through the planting of churches over a wide area. The classic case for Paul was the Ephesian ministry. He spent more time in Ephesus than in any single city. He could say after a period of three years there that "all who lived in Asia heard the word of the Lord, both Jews and Greeks" (Acts 19:10). This was Paul's method, and it works today.

This does not mean the church should avoid ministry where few people reside. As a case in point, the illustration of Dr. Robert Jackson makes that clear. Jackson's rural church finally went worldwide. William Carey ministered in India seven years before winning his first convert; but this approach eventually opened up all of India to the gospel. The vision and target strategy is what matters. From whatever point we start, there can be a reaching out until finally we touch the whole world. But of course, if we have a strong base in a large urban area, this usually makes that task easier. Still, the small church must not "give up" because of its size. God uses people of vision no matter where they are or how large their constituency may be. God can do miracles anywhere. The point is to find God's will and then do it.

Paul, above all, planted and organized churches. The kingdom progresses best in the establishment of new congregations. Then Paul raised up leaders to guide those new churches. In his admonition to Titus, the leader of the church in Crete, Paul said: "For this reason I left you in Crete, that you might set in order what remains, and appoint elders in every city as I directed you" (Titus 1:5). Churches should be properly organized and staffed. The church that grows demands leaders. Ecclesiastical structures of diverse churches and denominations obviously differ from one another. Nevertheless, the structure that follows biblical principles as closely as possible and allows God's Spirit to raise up leadership functions best. Every congregation can fashion its organizational structures in such a way that God-called leaders can lead and equip the entire body of believers to exercise their spiritual gift as the work goes forward. This opens the door to another important principle equipping the church.

We have emphasized how the Spirit of God creates the ministering church in the bestowal of spiritual gifts. God's people get involved in the task of evangelism when they discover their spiritual gift, begin to function on this basis, and share Jesus Christ with others. This is how the principles of spiritual gifts and evangelization go hand in glove. Equipping the church on this principle is essential for good church growth. Revival coupled with good methodologies spells evangelism, and evangelism means church growth.

This points to the importance of permitting the Spirit of God to create what has been called "the full-service church"—our next consideration.

TEN QUESTIONS FOR STUDY

1. What is the meaning of *evangelism?*
2. How does evangelism "fit" in the *missio dei?*
3. What are the principles for doing effective evangelism?
4. What is the content of our evangelistic message?
5. What does it mean to contextualize the gospel?
6. Is contextualization important? Why?
7. What are the lessons to learn from the essence of the gospel?
8. What obstacles must be overcome in the worldwide mission of the gospel?
9. How did Jesus do evangelism?
10. What has evangelism to do with revival and church growth?

CHAPTER 7

THE FULL-SERVICE CHURCH IN SPIRITUAL AWAKENING AND CHURCH GROWTH

The eighteenth century was a time of significant church growth and expansion in the American colonies. It happened as a consequence of the First Great Awakening. The movement traveled up and down the East Coast on the wings of the preaching of spiritual giants such as Jonathan Edwards, Gilbert Tennant, Theodore Frelingheusen, and a host of others. The same thing was happening in Britain through leaders like John Wesley and George Whitefield. Even the continent of Europe felt the impact. The Spirit of God moved the established and dissenting believers alike. Churches on both sides of the Atlantic experienced a transformation, and many new congregations were planted as a result of the revival.

These churches began to minister with a relevancy to their contemporary culture, the like of which had not been seen for many years. In the parlance of current church-growth writers, they became "full-service" churches. People's genuine needs were addressed.

This principle of church life and ministry sets the ideal for all congregations. But notice that the new spirit and approach of those churches came hard on the heels of a sweeping spiritual awakening. Revivals invariably instill such a spirit of service. The full-service church emerges out of a spiritually healthy church, and this health comes about by spiritual awakening. How does the full-service church minister?

THE FULL-SERVICE CHURCH

We do not have to search very far to find the ideal pattern for the full-service congregation. The first-century church ministered in this fashion. We read in Acts 2:44–45, "All those who had believed were together, and had all things in common; and they began selling their property and possessions, and were sharing them with all, as anyone might have need." As a result, "The Lord was adding to their number day by day those who were being saved" (v. 47).

Another example is in the feeding of the needy widows recorded in Acts 6:1–7. We know that such action not only aided the widows; it also gave rise to a new leadership structure in the life of the church and significant increase in membership. Luke tells us, "The word of God kept on spreading; and the number of the disciples continued to increase greatly in Jerusalem, and a great many of the priests were becoming obedient to the faith" (v. 7). The specific needs of the congregation were being cared for, and it had a positive spin-off in growth.

Such an approach to ministry became the pattern of the apostolic church. The followers of Jesus emulated their Lord in those early years. Taking their lead from Jesus, they healed the sick, cast out demons, fed the hungry, and met the multiplicity of needs that pressed upon them. And they structured the life of the church in such a fashion that relevant needs could be met in a manner that involved the entire membership. The great missionary evangelist Paul was vitally concerned to raise money to relieve the poverty of the saints in Jerusalem. The apostle John laid down the challenge: "We know love by this, that He laid down His life for us; and we ought to lay down our lives for the brethren. But whoever has the world's goods, and beholds his brother in need and closes his heart against him, how does the love of God abide in him?" (1 John 3:16–17). This principle becomes the practical application of the principle of the Holy Spirit creating his "fruit" and the bestowal of spiritual gifts of ministry. And people will respond.

BACKGROUNDS

There are many historical and contemporary examples of this approach to ministry. We need only look at the dynamics of the British church scene at the same time as America's First Great Awakening. The Wesley Chapel that still exists in London is a paradigm for this understanding of ministry. Wesley himself became something of the inspiration for the chapel ministry. The gospel was proclaimed. Benevolent work abounded. Even prison reform was established. Wesley's church reached beyond the immediate environs of its own community.

In the nineteenth century, evangelist Charles Finney, after becoming professor of theology and president at Oberlin College, revolutionized Christian education. All admire Finney's commitment to evangelism and church growth, but his approach to ministry developed a full-service congregation that stands as a sterling example. Not many know that Oberlin, through the ministry of Finney and his congregation (he served as pastor of the campus church), actually became a key northern railhead of the so-called "underground railroad." Large numbers of slaves that escaped their southern masters, making their way north, flowed through the channel that Finney created.

This was just one facet of Finney's ministry approach. Oberlin became the first college to go coeducational; he also admitted students of all races as a first-time venture. He even created a physical health program in the college. They had a dietary plan. The menu did not sound very appetizing. It consisted primarily of gruel. But everyone thrived on it. Finney's ministry extended to the multiple needs of the people he served. He exemplified Christ's concern to meet all needs through his church and college.

Many contemporary churches are also committed to reaching people in the multiplicity of life's situations. Perhaps one of the most captivating examples of this full-service approach is the Saddleback

Community Church in Orange County, California. Pastor Rick Warren has created an incredible, well-rounded ministry of service to the community. As you walk out of the huge but simple building, you face a series of booths. Each booth provides a place where church members can get information and "sign up" to engage in specific ministries they feel gifted to exercise. These ministries include spiritual life development, evangelism, and social needs. The challenge is put before the congregation to meet the total needs of the total community.

The Saddleback Community Church has proven that a church does not need elaborate buildings and structures to create a dynamic ministry. In the twenty or so years of its existence, the church has moved to more than a dozen different rental locations. The church finally settled down at the present site, but even there they do not have an ornate building. Yet thousands of people come every Saturday and Sunday to worship and then throw themselves into community service through the life of their church. We tend to think we must have many things to establish a full-service type of ministry. All it really takes is vision and people—a people committed to serve Jesus Christ on a genuine biblical basis. God has been able to use Rick Warren to accomplish just that, and the results are phenomenal.

One of the tragedies of the early twentieth century, especially in America, was that it saw the diminution of this full-service approach, precipitated by the so-called "modernist-fundamentalist" controversy. The "modernists" were concerned about what came to be known as the "social gospel"—meeting the social needs of people. At the same time, unfortunately, many of these churches downplayed concern for the evangelization of people as their evangelical theology deteriorated. It must be granted that the theology of some was questionable.

A conservative pastor in 1953 condemned the social gospel movement on four theological points: (1) the doctrine of God (the social gospel questioned his sovereignty); (2) the doctrine of man (some held all people are already children of God—the heresy of universalism); (3) the doctrine of sin (it was argued that sin must be seen no longer as a "black curse"); (4) the doctrine of social order (they believed a golden age is coming).[1] Some of these positions have faded in recent years. Still, evangelism all but died in several churches.

In reaction to these views, the fundamentalists, or conservative evangelicals, who understood the centrality and the priority of evangelization, equated a diminution of evangelistic commitment and evangelical theology with social action. Thus, they gave themselves almost exclusively to seeing people brought to faith in Christ as they reacted to the modernist's motif of the faith. This was a tragedy—for both sides. The earlier nineteenth-century church knew little of this separation. Evangelical theology, evangelistic commitment, and social action were kept together in beautiful harmony. But it came apart in the early twentieth century, and the entire body of Christ suffered as a result. This problem seems to be fading today. Many contemporary churches have become more holistic in their ministry approach. As a consequence, they are developing full-service churches.

The full-service church ideal can make a positive contribution to the furtherance of God's kingdom. This approach doesn't take a lot of resources. All it takes is a biblical view of meeting needs and a spiritually healthy congregation. How does it work?

MOVING THE CHURCH FORWARD

Most congregations will require a significant move of the Holy Spirit before the membership can be enlisted to meet the needs of people in a holistic fashion. But as the Spirit begins to motivate believers, the first step is to understand community needs. This must not be done with a hit-or-miss approach. The church must come to grips with what the community needs.

AN EXAMPLE

A good example of understanding community needs emerged in the early ministry of Robert Schuller at the Garden Grove

Community Church in south Los Angeles. Whether one agrees with all of Schuller's approach or understanding of ministry, it must be granted that he struck a sound note in his early days as he attempted to uncover the needs of Orange County.

Dr. Schuller went to southern California as a young pastor after serving a short time in Chicago, Illinois. With his family, pulling an organ in a trailer and with five hundred dollars from the Dutch Reformed Church denomination, he traveled west to plant a new church. When Schuller arrived in Orange County, he first had to find a venue to commence the work. All possible space such as the Masonic Hall, the funeral home chapel, and schools were taken by Baptists, Presbyterians, Methodists, and other groups attempting to get a work started. He was discouraged, but he finally received an invitation from the Orange Drive-In Theater to use their facilities. He preached from the roof of the concession stand of the old drive-in movie theater as people came and sat in their cars to listen. This was innovative in itself. It put him on the wavelength of people who were accustomed in those days to drive-in theaters. But how could a full-service church be developed out of that? Then he hit on an idea.

Schuller decided he would visit everybody in the community. In his first year of ministry, he actually knocked on the doors of three thousand homes. He averaged ten calls a day, excluding Sunday. It was a Herculean task, but he undertook it and accomplished it. He would introduce himself as Robert Schuller, pastor of the Garden Grove Community Church. He learned right away not to call it the Dutch Reformed Church because there were very few Dutch Reformed people in the area. He would then ask the question, "What would you like the Garden Grove Community Church to do for you?" If he got a sensible answer that expressed a genuine need, he would reply, "We are a very young church and we do not have the resources to meet that need yet. However, as soon as we are able to meet that need, we will be back and minister to you as we can."

In that fashion, he learned the genuine needs of the community and coined his famous phrase, "Finding hurts and healing them."

That became something of the purpose statement of the Garden Grove Church as they geared their church life on the basis of what they discovered as "hurts" in their community. A few years back Schuller was able to announce (this author heard him on television) that the needs the community expressed in those early days were now being fully met. He saw it as a day of triumph.

An interesting sidelight came out of Schuller's program that significantly affected his preaching. One day in that first year he knocked on a door and introduced himself to a woman. She immediately said, "I'm Jewish." She was about to slam the door, but he stopped her and said, "Wait a minute. I'm going to preach on Abraham this coming Sunday. You should be interested in that." The lady retorted, "Who?" He replied, "Abraham." She shot back, "Who in the world is Abraham?" Schuller explained that he was the father of the Jewish people. The woman, somewhat surprised, asked, "Where did you find that out?" Schuller replied, "Well, in the Bible, in the Old Testament Scriptures, the Jewish holy writings." The lady replied, "Well, I've heard something about the Bible. I might be there." And then she did slam the door.

The very next Sunday morning, right in the front row of cars where Schuller could clearly see her, sat that Jewish lady. He looked at his notes (not that the notes and the theology they expressed were wrong) and wondered how he was going to communicate effectively to her from his Dutch Reformed background. The way he traditionally expressed himself would probably miss her by a thousand miles. He later confessed, "That changed my style of preaching." He learned to get on the wavelength of a very diverse community.

This approach, in principle, wins the game. Although we would find it difficult in most communities to visit door to door, there are ways of discovering community needs. The issue becomes doing in principle what Schuller did, finding hurts in the community that the church can heal. It begins with a systematic, sympathetic approach. Hit-and-miss methods will not accomplish the task. Growing churches do it right.

GREAT GROWING CHURCHES

Church growth expert Elmer Towns investigated ten booming churches across America. Each church had a different approach to its ministry, but each had found the key to reaching the community with its needs for Christ. The Perimeter Church in Atlanta, Georgia, discovered the need for a multiplicity of meeting points, so they developed a ring of churches around the Atlanta area. The New Hope Community Church in Portland, Oregon, has an effective cell ministry. People are brought together in small groups, reminiscent of the Pietistic-Wesleyan approach of reaching people.

New innovative ways to worship are undertaken today by the Willow Creek Community Church in South Barrington, Illinois. The well-known pastor, Bill Hybels, has been a pacesetter in reaching the Boomer generation for Christ. Now he is designing an approach to reach out to the Busters. Even the older traditional methods are at times effective. A case in point is the First Baptist Church of Jacksonville, Florida. Its type of ministry reaches many people in the culture of the Deep South. Illustrations can be multiplied. Fresh forms of worship, a new awareness of where people are in their lives, home, family, and work becomes absolutely vital. The innovative church can step in to such situations and develop an effective ministry.

PRIORITIES

At the same time, it is essential that priorities be kept in place. Proper prioritizing emerges on a threefold level.

First, the members must be committed to spiritual growth. As George Barna, a leading church growth authority, has said:

> I long to see revival wash this land of its wayward leanings and evil choices. I desperately want to help expose myths about evangelism and church outreach that stop us from having an impact. I passionately want to encourage the "average" Christian to understand that each of us has a vital part to play in the transformation of our hearts and culture . . . this book may be a needed wake-up call; get into the game and share

the Good News, now! For others it may be a needed wake-up call of another kind: Understand the fields that are ripe for the harvest and act intelligently and strategically.[2]

What George Barna is saying revolves around the issue that commitment and spiritual growth must become the first priority of the full-service church. If we need revival, let us seek it at all costs and give it top priority. Just as Jehosophat put the choir in front of the army as God's forces engaged the enemy (2 Chron. 20:20–30), may we place the spiritual priorities first. Then we, too, may see a victory as did Israel of old.

A second priority is that God's people must be challenged, equipped, and thrust out to reach the challenging generations with the eternal gospel of Jesus Christ. No matter how deep—or shallow—their spiritual commitment at the moment may be, the church must train and challenge its members to share Christ. We should never forget that biblical evangelism culminates in making disciples. Moreover, we must never compromise the gospel in order to be "relevant" to our communities. All this will require overcoming many obstacles. But we press on.

OVERCOMING

In his excellent book, *Evangelism That Works,* George Barna lists thirteen obstacles to effective evangelism that must be conquered:

1. The absence of prayer. The Bible admonishes God's people to prevail in prayer.
2. Owning outreach. Church members must realize that the central mission and ministry of the church is a personal responsibility.
3. Building bridges. Aiding the people to reach across all cultural, economic, and racial barriers to address the lost with the gospel of Christ.
4. Seeking the right outcome. Leading the church to seek not more decisions, but genuine conversions to a life of discipleship.
5. The pastor's role. The pastor must provide effective leadership in every dimension of ministry activity, including evangelism.

6. Developing standards. Establishing the goals and objectives of the church and clearly setting them forth.

7. Hardening of the arteries. Eliminating programs that are no longer effective.

8. Open the door wide. Use all possible methods to address unbelievers with the gospel of Christ; do not rely upon just one methodology.

9. Bad ministry. Americans are in the frame of mind where high quality performance must attend anything to which they will give their time and interest. The church cannot afford to be an exception.

10. Preparing the saints for the task. Equipping God's people to become witnesses for Christ.

11. Responsibility with authority. If believers have the responsibility to evangelize, they must be given the authority to do so.

12. Inter-church unity. There must be love and harmony among the people of God.

13. Celebration of victories. To fail to celebrate victories is to fail to honor God and give him praise for his mighty works. This discourages the congregation as well.[3]

All these obstacles must be honestly addressed and overcome. Evangelism for discipleship is foundational in the church. When we overcome barriers, God's people are released for ministry. This comes from spiritual vitality.

A third priority in the full-service church is social ministry. The full-service church fulfills in service the full needs of the community as resources are available. But this leads to the next important point. After the priorities are set in place and we have a sense of what the needs are, we must do effective programming for ministry.

PROGRAMMING FOR MINISTRY

Many churches do not take thoughtful programming as seriously as they ought. It is essential that relevant programs be instituted and developed and that they fall in line with the purpose statement of the church.

The church must be equipped for the task of implementing the programs. Christian ministry is not easy. Jesus said, "My yoke is easy, and My load is light" (Matt. 11:30), but this does not mean there is no hard work involved in the Christian faith. It certainly does not mean that we should ignore equipping workers for the tasks that need to be done. Churches that grow set about to train workers and then thrust them out into the fields ripe for harvest. In this way members of the congregation learn the thrill of serving Christ effectively. God's people need equipping for the task. This makes for a successful full-service church.

This leads to the "five-point pattern" of programming and gearing the church for the ministry the Holy Spirit leads his people to undertake:

1. The church has a written statement of purpose. The church must see to it that its purpose is biblical, Christ-honoring, and people-centered and that it is done for the praise of Christ in kingdom extension. The *mission dei* becomes the foundation of the exercise. Then the church must rise to the challenge. But motivation comes essentially from the Holy Spirit; therefore, we should pray much.

2. The next job centers in developing programs that will fulfill the church's stated purpose. These programs are to be based on the church's statement of purpose, and they should emerge out of community needs.

3. Then goals are set for fulfilling these programs. Goals should be challenging, attainable, and measurable.

4. People must be enlisted and equipped to meet these goals in actual ministry. They are to be chosen for their roles on the basis of their spiritual gifts.

5. Continuous evaluation is the final step. Programs must be constantly evaluated on the basis of the four principles outlined above. These questions should be regularly raised: Is our pur-

pose statement right? Is the program to reach that purpose statement based on the Bible and community needs, and is it still relevant? Moreover, we should ask if the goals are sensible and realistic and if God's people in the task are being better equipped constantly for their ministry. Finally, ask if this evaluation is honest, objective, and remedial in that it keeps the church on track.

These principles may sound somewhat like the "Madison Avenue" approach, but truth is truth. If these interpersonal dynamics are operative in human encounters and relationships—whether it be in the business world or in the spiritual realm—they are still true. All truth stems from God. Therefore, we should serve him on the basis of all aspects of truth and be "wise as serpents, and harmless as doves" (Matt. 10:16 KJV). These principles function best when the church is in a state of spiritual health.

CONCLUSION

The full-service church works to God's glory in meeting needs. We should use wise, relevant, and ethical methods—recognizing that wisdom comes from God—and throw ourselves into the work of seeing this needy world redeemed and its needs met. When God's people assume this beautiful balance, great things happen. The Bible is balanced on this point; why not the church?

We turn now to consider the place of the Scriptures in this grand enterprise of spiritual awakening and church growth.

TEN QUESTIONS FOR STUDY

1. What is a full-service church?

2. Why is a full-service church important?

3. Does a spiritual awakening contribute to developing a full-service church? How?

4. Is the full-service church a new concept? What are its roots? Is it biblical?

5. What has such a church to do with the spiritual health of a congregation?

6. What is the balance between social ministries and evangelism?

7. How are effective service ministries developed?

8. How do full-service ministries contribute to church growth?

9. How does one keep priorities straight?

10. What obstacles must be overcome in developing a full-service church, and how is such a church created?

CHAPTER 8

THE WORD OF GOD IN SPIRITUAL AWAKENING AND CHURCH GROWTH

The genuineness of any spiritual movement depends on its conformity to the Word of God. As has been implied throughout this book, a local body of believers immersed in the Scriptures makes the most significant impact for growth to the glory of God and his kingdom. Spiritual awakening, church growth, and the Bible are inseparable. The Scriptures themselves proclaim this essential truth:

For the word of God is living and active and sharper than any two-edged sword, and piercing as far as the division of soul and spirit, of both joints and marrow, and able to judge the thoughts and intentions of the heart. (Heb. 4:12)

For it is sanctified by means of the word of God and prayer. (1 Tim. 4:5)

Take THE HELMET OF SALVATION, and the sword of the Spirit, which is the word of God. (Eph. 6:17)

So faith comes from hearing, and hearing by the word of Christ. (Rom. 10:17)

Now it came about that while the multitude were pressing around Him (Jesus) and listening to the word of God. (Luke 5:1)

The grass withers, the flower fades, but the word of our God stands forever. (Isa. 40:8)

The Word of God undergirds the total work of God. No church will genuinely grow from a kingdom perspective until it comes alive to this reality and begins to gear its entire life on that basis.

THE USE OF THE BIBLE

In Psalm 119 we read how the Scriptures become central when used by the Holy Spirit in the spiritually awakened believer:

Incline my heart to Thy testimonies,
And not to dishonest gain.
Turn away my eyes from looking at vanity,
And revive me in Thy ways. . . .
Behold, I long for Thy precepts;
Revive me through Thy righteousness. . . .
This is my comfort in my affliction,
That Thy word has revived me. (vv. 36–37, 40, 50)

The Word of God does its work in reviving the church and thus thrusting it into its ministry of worldwide evangelization and kingdom growth. A captivating illustration of this reality can be found in Acts 4 when persecution first fell on the early believers. Jewish officials arrested John and Peter, threw them in prison, threatened and then released them. The church gathered around the apostles and prayed earnestly. Then, "when they had prayed, the place where they had gathered together was shaken, and they were all filled with the Holy Spirit, and began to speak the word of God with boldness" (Acts 4:31). This boldness came as a result of the work of the Holy Spirit. Strengthened by the powerful Word of God, the church went forth to evangelize the world.

TIMELESS TESTIMONY

Through the years, God's people have experienced the same phenomenon countless times. In the turbulent fifteenth century, a few years before the Protestant Reformation burst on the scene, a dejected monk retreated to his little cell. He gave himself to the study of the Scriptures. This was not done very much in those days. The Word of God came alive to the monk. He could not get his eyes off the pages of the Book of Revelation. He saw in it the threatening judgments of God. He became convinced that doom would soon fall upon the nation unless the people repented and turned in true faith to Jesus Christ. He turned away from the legalism and forms of his church and began to proclaim the pure gospel. He preached three hundred sermons in St. Mark's Cathedral of Florence, Italy, from the Book of Revelation. Through the power of his preaching of the Word of God, people were overwhelmed by God's Spirit. One historian describes the scene in these words:

So large was the concourse gathered to hear him that he had to transfer himself to the Cathedral. Here, day after day, the population of Florence thronged to see and hear him. Many were drawn by curiosity, but even the most superficial became awed as they listened to the burning words of the preacher. The crowds thronged and pressed each other so close that there was hardly room to breathe; they built seats against the walls in the form of an amphitheater, and still the space was insufficient. And how is it possible at this date to describe the preacher? The deep resonant voice, the flash of his deep-set, penetrating eyes, the impassioned gestures, the marvelous flow of his oratory as, swept along with the fiery vehemence of his great soul, he discoursed to men of the eternal verities, of the awful facts of death and judgement to come? First he would begin in measured and tranquil tones, taking up the subject, turning it quietly round, suggesting some scholarly exposition, advancing some interpretation, dealing with it casually, critically, suggestively; then, suddenly, often without warning, he would change; the mediative style was flung aside as the mantle of the prophet fell upon him; fire flashed from his eyes, the thunder came into his voice; now in passionate entreaty, now in scorching indignation, the sentences rushed out, never halting, never losing intensity or volume, but growing and growing until his voice became as the voice of God Himself, and all the building rocked and swayed as if it were moved to the mighty passion of his words. And what of the hearers? They were as clay in his hands. Tears gushed from their eyes, they beat their breasts, they cried unto God for mercy, the church echoed and re-echoed with their sobs. Those who report his sermons suddenly break off and say: "Here was I so overcome with weeping that I could not go on." Pico della Mirandola, one of the most learned men of the day, says that the mere sound of his voice was as the clap of doom; a cold shiver ran through the marrow of his bones, the hairs of his head stood on end as he listened. Another tells that these sermons caused such terror, alarm, such sobbing and tears, that every one passed through the streets without speaking, more dead than alive.[1]

His name? Savanorola: precursor of the Reformation. But such power did not reside in Savanorola as a man; such incredible power could come only by the work of the Spirit of God taking the Word of God and communicating it through his surrendered servant.

The Scriptures were central in the lives of the Reformers who soon followed the monk of Florence. Through the study of Psalms, Galatians, and Romans, Martin Luther discovered that salvation comes by grace through faith, as did Calvin, Zwingi, and others. In this realization, the Reformation burst on the scene. We live in the light and the legacy of that blessed sixteenth-century revival to this day.

Our contemporary age is no exception to this rule. Great people of God still stand in pulpits and on street corners alike preaching the Bible. When they proclaim the Scriptures in the power of the Holy Spirit, marvelous things take place. Countless have been the occasions that evangelists like Charles Finney, D. L. Moody, and Billy Sunday attest to this truth. In the large amphitheaters and sports arenas around the world, Billy Graham still declares the Word of God. As he preaches Jesus Christ and his power to save, the simple biblical gospel strikes home to hearts in an incredible fashion. This writer has seen it many times. One can scarcely believe the response of people. But again, the power does not reside in Billy Graham or the great music or the mass psychology of the throngs. It rests, as Paul said, in the gospel itself (Rom. 1:16). If a revival with any depth and meaning comes, it will emerge out of the faithful communication, preaching, teaching, and sharing of the Scriptures. This alone will bring meaningful kingdom church growth.

Moreover, coming to grips with the Scripture spells rich spiritual growth for individuals as well. A graphic illustration recently came to this author. One of my former students serves as minister to college students in a local church. He has undertaken a Bible study program for the students he serves. Not long ago a twenty-year-old college student came to him to say how much she had been helped and strengthened through being immersed in an in-depth study of the Book of Mark. She related this was the first time she had ever been involved in such a spiritually rewarding program in her church. Her life had been spent in the heart of the church for years. She went on youth mission trips, choir tours, and such. But she said, "I am angry with my church; I have never really been taught the Word of God. No one ever shared like this before." Her life was transformed by serious study of the Scriptures.

This points up the necessity of solid teaching of God's Word for all God's people. The Bible does wonders in the hands of the Holy Spirit. What can we say about this book and its nature that may help us understand these principles better?

THE NATURE OF THE BIBLE

It all begins with Jesus' statement: "Thy word is truth" (John 17:17). The Bible is true because it comes to us inspired by the Holy Spirit—*totally* inspired by the Spirit, thus *totally* true. God reveals himself as the ultimate author. As Paul told Timothy: "All scripture is given by inspiration of God, and is profitable for doctrine, for reproof, for correction, for instruction in righteousness" (2 Tim. 3:16 KJV). This implies several principles.

A WORD OF AUTHORITY

God has spoken; therefore, we have an *authoritative* word. This means we are to *obey* its precepts. This biblical authority and resultant obedience applies not only to individuals but to the church as a body. As Dewey Beegle states, "Scripture becomes the basis of appeal in all matters pertaining to the content of faith and the practice of Christian living."[2] Billy Graham put it well when he wrote, "When we say that the Bible is authoritative, we mean it is God's binding revelation to us. We submit to it because it has come from God."[3] The Bible can be a channel or means to spawn revival.

An Instrument in Sanctification and Revival

God desires to create a holy lifestyle in his people. The word *holy* embraces a twofold meaning in the hands of the Spirit. First, it forms the core of what the Scriptures call sanctification (1 Thess. 4:3). The work of God in progressive sanctification means the Holy Spirit sets us apart *from sin*. The Spirit by the Word shows us our sin that we might experience cleansing in Christ's blood (1 John 1:9). On the positive side, we are "set apart" *to God*—to worship, serve, obey, and magnify him through a dedicated life. Jesus prayed, "Sanctify them in the truth; Thy word is truth" (John 17:17). Thus, the Word, applied by the Holy Spirit, does the work. When revival dawns on God's people, our Lord reveals himself as holy (Isa. 6:1–7). That inspires and challenges the church to purity, equipping believers by immersing them in the Word for powerful ministry. The Bible in the hands of the Holy Spirit can do wondrous things.

An Instrument of God's Leadership in the Growing Church

David prayed, "Open my eyes, that I may behold wonderful things from Thy law" (Ps. 119:18). The Bible, God's Law, holds the answer to all basic questions of life. By a daily, consistent lifting up of God's truth, a church can come to know God's plan and purpose and overcome its difficulties. Churches need to "search the Scriptures" (John 5:39) to find guidance and leadership in its ministry and to see the wonderful things the Bible promises.

An Instrument in Effective Christian Service

A grand old hymn of the faith states:
The service of Jesus, true pleasure affords;
In Him there is joy, without an alloy;

'Tis heaven to trust Him and rest on His words;
It pays to serve Jesus each day.

One of the pleasures of the Christian life centers in service exercised in Jesus' name through one's church. In such service, the Scripture becomes the most effective tool. Paul tells us in Ephesians 6:17 to take "the sword of the Spirit, which is the word of God." Strengthened by God's Word, God's people can achieve great victories for our Lord.

What more can be said about the Bible? It stands as God's instrument in all kingdom advance. The church must learn to use it wisely. Despite its critics and supposed problems, God's Word endures. Even the onslaught of secular critical science cannot diminish its voice. Concerning the Bible and the imagined conflict between science and the Scriptures, Sir Winston Churchill said:

When professors with high sounding titles attempt to palm off their pernicious denials of the Holy Scriptures by labeling them: "The Findings of Science" or "The Consensus of Scholarship," some folks take them seriously and are ready to throw away their Bibles. . . . We may be sure that all these things (what the Bible says) happened just as they are set out according to Holy Writ. We may believe that they happened to people not so very different from ourselves, and that the impressions those people received were faithfully recorded and have been transmitted across the centuries with far more accuracy than many of the telegraphed accounts we read of goings on of today. In the words of a forgotten work of Mr. Gladstone, we rest with assurance upon "THE IMPREGNABLE ROCK OF HOLY SCRIPTURE."[4]

It should be realized on both sides of the science-religion debate that the Bible does not deal with the question of whether the Big Bang theory of creation is correct. The Scriptures do not give us Newton's three laws of motion or Einstein's concept of relativity. Paul did not have a word processor when he wrote Romans. We must see the Bible for what it is: a book about God. We should not read into the

Scriptures things that cannot be found there. Nor is it fair for the scientific mind to commit the same error and create conflict. No problem arises between *true* science and *correct* Bible interpretation. Actually, they imply one another; after all, truth *is* truth.

Truth prevails wherever we may find it—in the laboratory or on our knees before an open Bible. We accept the Bible for what God claims it to be and refuse to argue for what it is not. And we ask the scientist or historian to take the same humble approach. We thank God that we have the Spirit-inspired Scriptures that give us a revelation of himself. Our minds and hearts need to humble themselves and submit to God and his Word. This will do much to eliminate problems and so-called contradictions in the Scriptures. The *humble* approach on all sides can resolve supposed conflicts. And it is not incidental that modern research in cosmology and quantum physics is beginning to demonstrate a striking affinity between the Scriptures and science, as previously pointed out.

It becomes clear why the Bible itself declares that it is the "sword of the Spirit." This sword in the hands of the Spirit works wonders. We can conclude with confidence that the Bible is the key instrument in all spiritual advance that brings lasting growth. But how do we implement the Bible in spiritual awakening and church growth?

PRINCIPLES FOR USING THE BIBLE

Several things can be said about the place of the Scriptures as the church attempts to reach the community. It all begins by God's people understanding and appreciating what the Bible actually is and what it can accomplish. These things we have already made clear, but God's people must develop a genuine confidence in the Bible to accomplish its task. Not only are appreciation and confidence needed; a love and heart hunger for the Word of God also should be generated in the Lord's people. The psalmist said the Word of God was "sweeter also than honey and the drippings of the honeycomb" (Ps. 19:10). It is also "a lamp to my feet, and a light to my path" (Ps. 119:105). The Bible sweetens the way and lightens the road as one treads the path of God's will. If the Word of

God can do this, the people of God must be led to appreciate its nature. We also need to incorporate its truth into our lives and to use it wisely.

A Discipline

These truths apply first on an individual, personal basis. The discipline of regular Scripture reading, study, and meditation should be ingrained in the believer. No Christian will grow in Christ and contribute to the progress of the kingdom of God until the Word of God holds a rightful place in his or her life. This demands disciplined study.

The Scriptures must also assume their proper role in the life of the church. Biblical exposition ought to be forthcoming from the pulpit and in teaching in the classroom. Of course, we must not fall into the pitfall of bibliolatry—worshiping the Bible—but we must grant the Scriptures their central role. They should be ingrained in the life of the body.

The classic example of revival through an in-depth scriptural emphasis can be found in the Puritan-Pietist movement. The effects of this movement are evident to this day because it was deeply committed to the Word of God. A similar lesson can be found in the Welsh Revival of 1904. In the Welsh movement, spiritual manifestations were tremendous. Great singing, wonderful testimonies, and praise services went on all night. Jubilation reigned among the people. However, in some aspects of the Welsh Revival, there was a dearth of biblical preaching and teaching. Many of the people were not rooted and grounded in the Word of God. Thus the revival was short-lived. Although many participants in this revival did persevere in their faith to the end of their lives, the churches soon emptied. But those Welsh folk who were revived in the context of more solid biblical preaching saw more lasting results.

We should heed this lesson from history. When awakening comes, we must keep the movement rooted, grounded, and saturated in the Word of God if we want a long-term, lasting impact. This establishes the foundation for the quality of growth we seek.

Assimilating God's Truth

Assimilating the Scripture emerges from a life that is yielded to its truth. As one person put it, "It is only the heart that yields to be led by the Holy Spirit that can expect to profit by the teaching of the

Word, and truly to know Christ in His divine saving power."[5] Recognizing the basic nature of the Spirit-inspired Scriptures, believers come to our Lord in *earnest prayer* before reading, praying the Spirit will interpret the Word to the heart and mind. Then, the prayer to receive grace to follow God's lead in all things arises in the heart. We sincerely ask the heavenly Father to guide us, open our minds, give us a responsive heart, and grant us grace and a revelation of himself by the power of the Holy Spirit. Paul wrote to the Corinthians: "As it is written, 'THINGS WHICH EYE HAS NOT SEEN AND EAR HAS NOT HEARD, and which HAVE NOT ENTERED THE HEART OF MAN, ALL THAT GOD HAS PREPARED FOR THOSE WHO LOVE HIM.' For to us God revealed them through the Spirit; for the Spirit searches all things, even the depths of God. . . . Now we have received, not the spirit of the world, but the Spirit who is from God, that we might know the things freely given to us by God" (1 Cor. 2:9–10, 12).

The church must depend on the Spirit of God to give it strength to yield to its demands. The Spirit alone can enlighten the heart and mind with grace to obey. Keith Wiginton expressed it well: "The same Holy Spirit who inspired the Bible indwells every believer to illumine the mind and heart so that we can appreciate and appropriate the Word of God into our lives."[6]

So the Bible becomes the staple of God's people. A converted cannibal was seen one day seated on a log reading his Bible as a European trader passed by. The European asked him what he was doing.

"Reading the Bible," he replied.

"That book is out-of-date in my country," said the trader.

"If it had been out-of-date here," said the ex-cannibal, "you would have been eaten long ago."

God transforms us through the Word of truth. Andrew Murray said the church has to be "full of the conviction that Scripture is indeed God's word; that God Himself, through His Spirit, spoke in the prophets, and that it has the power of God dwelling in it."[7] The Bible is the kind of book that releases the power of God and spawns revival.

All of this implies that the Word of God inspires renewal and church growth as ministered in the power of the Holy Spirit. This is why Paul admonished the Ephesian church to "be filled with the Spirit" (Eph. 5:18). Spirit-filled, revived believers grow churches by sharing the Word of God with the world. Predicated upon these spiritual principles, church growth methodologies begin to take on a relevance that legitimizes the endeavor to further the life of the church. A few basic principles guide in the enterprise.

ENHANCING THE CHURCH

Only ethical methods of growth should be employed. They should be based on the Scriptures. Questionable practices must be avoided. Anything that would violate ethical, moral, or biblical principles is to be rejected. We serve a holy God. There should never be any question about the integrity of our methodologies.

In addition, the truth of the Word of God must never be compromised. Some truths from the Scriptures are repugnant to the world. Some realities of the Christian experience will be rejected by some unbelievers. The gospel always contains an element of "scandal." The church must be willing to bear this reproach, even though it may mean sacrifice, ridicule, and rejection by those we try to reach. Everyone will not respond to the gospel. Therefore, the church must be willing to make sacrifices, even at the cost of numerical growth.

On the other hand, we can rest assured that the Word of God will do its work. The Bible penetrates the hearts of people, bringing them to conviction and conversion. Let us have faith and permit its truth to accomplish its task wherever God sends it. We have his promise: "So shall My word be which goes forth from My mouth; it will not return to Me empty, without accomplishing what I desire, and without succeeding in the matter for which I sent it" (Isa. 55:11). With reliance upon God's Word, our faith commitment will be honored by the Lord.

Finally, the church must learn to communicate the Bible with relevance. We find ourselves in a rapidly changing society. We are being ushered into what has become known as the "postmodern" era. The old way of thinking, the system of values, and even what constitutes truth is in flux. Space does not permit us to go into the dynamics of this mentality. But wise is the church that comes to grips with the younger generations and learns to share the gospel convincingly with them. The Spirit of God always operates among his people and will show them how to communicate the Scriptures with relevance.

CONCLUSION

The future of the church rests upon the Word of God being shared in such a way that it comes alive to the mind-set of contemporary society. The matter can be summarized in what the psalmist said when he prayed, "Revive me, O LORD, according to Thy word" (Ps. 119:107). When this happens, the field becomes ripe for the harvest and church growth explodes.

Another major discipline in the spiritual experience of awakening and church growth—the centrality of prayer—must be addressed. To that we now turn.

TEN QUESTIONS FOR STUDY

1. What does the Bible say about itself?
2. What do scholars say about the Bible, and what do these things mean?
3. How does one relate the Bible to daily life?
4. Why do we say the Bible is authoritative?
5. What does *authority* mean in living the Christian life?
6. How does the Bible figure in a spiritual awakening?
7. What role does the Bible play in Christian service and subsequent church growth?
8. What personal disciplines in regard to the Bible are essential? What principles of interpretation are to be used?
9. How is God's Word assimilated in one's life?
10. How does the Bible relate to purifying the church and making the church a powerful witness, thus growing the church?

CHAPTER 9

THE MINISTRY OF PRAYER IN SPIRITUAL AWAKENING AND CHURCH GROWTH

Reference has been made to the effective ministry of Charles Haddon Spurgeon (1834–1892) in Victorian England. Few preachers have had a lasting prominence and influence for over a century as has Spurgeon. Although he could not boast of an extensive formal education, the success of his ministry has amazed multitudes worldwide. In the thirty-seven years of Spurgeon's London ministry, God honored the work. From a mere handful of people in his early days, he saw the congregation grow into a great megachurch. Explosive church growth occurred throughout his nearly four decades of ministry. What was his secret?

THE SECRET

Virtually every avenue has been traveled in an attempt to explain the Spurgeon epic. Many people attribute his success to his incredible preaching gifts. Others cite his great social ministry. Still others lift up his church-planting ministry and the itinerant evangelism in which he engaged. Yet good preaching, fine social ministries, and church-planting efforts have occurred for centuries and still explosive growth has not necessarily occurred. What happened in Spurgeon's ministry that made it so different? The great Victorian preacher wrote in the introduction to one of his volumes of sermons: "For six years the dew has never ceased to fall, and the rain has never been withheld. At this time the converts are more numerous than heretofore, and the zeal of the church growth exceedingly."[1] And what was the secret behind this moving of the Spirit? Revival born of prayer. The perceptive Spurgeon said:

When I came to New Park Street Chapel it was but a mere handful of people to whom I first preached, yet I could never forget how earnestly they prayed. Sometimes they seemed to plead as though they could really see the Angel of the Covenant present with them, and as if they must have a blessing from him. More than once we were all so awe-struck with the solemnity of the meeting that we sat silent for some moments while the Lord's Power appeared to overshadow us; and all I could do on such occasions was to pronounce the benediction, and say "Dear friends, we have had the Spirit of God here very manifestly tonight; let us go home and take care not to lose His gracious influence." Then down came the blessing; the house was filled with hearers. And many souls were saved.[2]

Few biographies of Spurgeon have recognized this aspect of his powerful ministry. Spurgeon found himself in the grip of a prayer-induced spiritual awakening. When he assumed the pastorate of New Park Street Baptist Church, later to become known as the Metropolitan Tabernacle, revival blessings fell. And he knew how to carry it on through the Word of God and the prayer of faith. He said, "Sound doctrine and loving invitation make a good basis of material, which, when modeled by the hand of prayer and faith, will form sermons of far more value in the saving of souls that the most philosophic essays prepared elaborately, and delivered with eloquence and propriety."[3]

Spurgeon became something of the English epitome of the Prayer Revival of 1858 that began in America and then crossed the Atlantic and began to move throughout the British countryside. But Spurgeon had already tasted a touch of revival before it broke out over Britain. Spiritual awakening became the primary key to the explosive growth of Spurgeon's church and made his London field ripe for the harvest.

We have learned from Spurgeon and a host of others that revival comes about essentially through prayer. One Lord's day, while declaring the gospel, Spurgeon cried out to the people, "Can you recollect how you prayed that God would fill this place with His glory? And how God has been with us ever since?"[4] The fervent prayers of the church precipitated the revival crest upon which he rode. One perceptive biographer said that Spurgeon "yearned over this city—we can best discover it in his prayers, in such a collection of his public prayers . . . Time and time again he prayed to Almighty God and wrestled with Him for the sinful city of London. As Paul was concerned for Rome, so Spurgeon was concerned for London." Spurgeon recognized that there has never been a great spiritual awakening without persistent, prevailing prayer. Prayer and spiritual awakening and church growth are bound up in the bundle of God's grace.

THE CENTRALITY OF PRAYER

One need go no further than the Scriptures to see the principle of prayer as paramount in church growth. The Old Testament is laced with fervent prayer that brought revival. When the prophets called the people to renewal and the perceptive leaders brought the nation together in the "solemn assemblies," prayer predominated. The prophet Habakkuk cried out: "LORD, I have heard the report about Thee and I fear. O LORD, revive Thy work in the midst of the years, in the midst of the years make it known; in wrath remember mercy. God comes from Teman, and the Holy One from Mount Paran. Selah. His splendor covers the heavens, and the earth is full of His praise" (Hab. 3:2–3).

All the prophets and psalmists lifted up their voices for revival. The psalmist prayed:

Wilt Thou not Thyself revive us again,
That Thy people may rejoice in Thee?
Show us Thy lovingkindness, O LORD,
And grant us Thy salvation. . . .
Righteousness will go before Him,
And will make His footsteps into a way.
(Ps. 85:6–7, 13)

When we come to the New Testament, the principle of prayer blossoms. Jesus Christ stands as the classic example. He would pray all night (Luke 6:12). He lifted up his voice in prayer and Lazarus was lifted up from the dead (John 11:43). Jesus pleaded with the Father as he was about to go to the cross, and God saw him through the ordeal (Luke 22:42). Jesus interceded for his disciples, and this prayer is being answered to this day (John 17). If such praying were necessary for Jesus, how much more so for us?

The New Testament church in its growth followed this same pattern. The day of Pentecost saw three thousand people saved in a matter of hours. But this day was preceded by ten days of prayer, fasting, and confession. When the Jewish leaders imprisoned Peter and his martyrdom seemed inevitable, the church prayed earnestly. God sent an angel to open the prison doors, and the Lord's faithful servant escaped (Acts 12). The apostle Paul pleaded with the churches to pray for him so an open door might be set before him to declare the gospel (Col. 4:2–4). The Scriptures are full of such accounts.

The great epics of church history repeat the same theme. One of the giants of the Middle Ages was the godly Francis of Assisi. He first encountered the Lord in fervent prayer at the little chapel of St. Domian. He met Jesus Christ in a vital, saving way, and God transformed his life. He went on to become a praying man of God. And he brought revival, even into the Roman Catholic Church. All of Italy as well as much of southern Europe felt the impact.

Martin Luther's prayer life was very disciplined. If he had an exceptionally hectic day and fell behind in his prayer time, he would always make up for it the next day. We think of Luther as the fiery Reformer who cried before his accusers, "Here I stand, I can do no other, God help me." We think of him as a great theologian and translator of the Bible. All this is true, but Luther was first of all a man of prayer. Under his leadership, the revival known as the Reformation swept Europe and eventually the world.

The eighteenth-century British Awakening and the fantastic growth of the church are no exceptions to this rule. One can visit the home where John Wesley lived during his years of revival ministry. In the house is one little room, no more than eight feet square, with just one small piece of furniture: his kneeling bench. John Wesley could be found early every morning spending two hours on his knees on that kneeling bench, pleading for the continuation of God's reviving power.

While the great revival swept the British countryside, a similar movement was occurring in America. We have all heard about Jonathan Edwards and the Whitefield ministry in America's First Great Awakening. One of the significant men of God, a man used powerfully by the Holy Spirit in those days, was David Brainerd. Deeply burdened for the Native Americans, he gave himself to agonizing prayer for their conversion. See him on his knees in deep snow, wet with perspiration from intercession, coughing blood from tubercular lungs, crying out to Christ for the conversion of the American Indians. He said, "I cared not where or how I lived or what hardships I went through so that I could but gain souls for Christ. While I was asleep I dreamed of these things, and when I awoke the first thing I thought of was this great work. All of my desire was for the conversion of the heathen and my hope was in God."

The Holy Spirit rewarded this spirit. Brainerd gives the account of how revival blessing fell: "The power of God seemed to descend upon the assembly 'like a rushing, mighty wind' and with an astonishing energy bore down on all before it. I stood amazed at the influence that seized the audience almost universally and could compare it to nothing more aptly than the irresistible force of a mighty torrent . . . . Almost all persons of all ages were bowed down with concern together, and scarce one was able to withstand the shock of this surprising operation."[5] Some historians have accused Brainerd of being neurotic. If that total dedication to prayer and evangelism is neurosis, may God so afflict all Christians.

As we move into the nineteenth century, giants like George Muller of England come to mind. He was one of the greatest people of faith that God ever gave to the world. His faith shone with a divine radiance. He housed, fed, and educated thousands of street urchins who would have been social castaways if not for Muller. His great faith enabled him to sustain the orphanage; and it all came about through his fervent prayers. He never solicited funds; he simply laid the needs before God. Our Lord met every need.

Early one morning, a worker knocked on Muller's door. "We must keep the children in bed this morning," he said. "There is not one bit of food in the entire orphanage. We have nothing for breakfast. We dare not get the children up."

Muller jumped out of bed and said, "Get them up, dressed, and bring them into the dining room." "But Mr. Muller," the servant replied, "we have no food."

"Get them up and get them assembled," Muller retorted.

The helper obeyed, got the children dressed, cleaned up, and assembled in the dining room. They sat down at the table. George Muller walked in, took his usual place at the head table, bowed his head, and thanked God for the wonderful breakfast they were about to enjoy. But there was not a morsel anywhere. When the "amen" fell from Muller's lips, the doors of the dining room burst open and a host of people came in carrying all sorts of food. And the children ate well that day. It was not planned; it was prayed for. It was not instigated; it was interceded for. God hears the prayer of faith.

In the twentieth century, perhaps the classic example of what prayer can do to bring multitudes to Christ is seen in the life of an American missionary. John Hyde graduated from the McCormick Theological Seminary in Chicago, Illinois. He made his way to the west coast to set sail for India; he had dedicated his life as a missionary to that "subcontinent of misery." As he was leaving, a friend handed him a letter. He tucked it in his coat pocket, went down to his stateroom, and settled in.

Remembering the letter later, John pulled it out and began to read. It was a short note from an old preacher friend. It asked, "Dear John, are you filled with the Holy Spirit? Your friend." The message did not sit too well with young John. *Think,* he said to himself, *I have dedi-*

cated my life to the mission field, and I've graduated from seminary, and I'm on my way to India. What does that old man mean, am I filled with the Spirit? Actually, it angered him to the point that he crumpled the letter, flung it on the stateroom floor, and paced out on the deck—and paced and paced and paced. God's convicting barb had pierced his proud young heart deeply.

Finally, God broke John's heart. When the young missionary stepped on the coral sands of India's shores, he was a different man than he had been when he left the United States. Through the years, God gave John Hyde one of the most unusual missionary ministries that India has ever seen. The Holy Spirit fashioned the new missionary into a great prayer warrior. Through the years of missionary service, his prayer life deepened until he was praying four hours a day. But God was also granting him, by the prayer of faith, four Indians won to Christ every day as well.

John became quite ill. He went to a doctor and was thoroughly examined. "What are you doing to yourself?" the doctor exclaimed, "What stress and strain are you putting yourself under? Never have I examined a heart in such terrible condition as yours. What are you up to?" John died not long afterwards of a brain tumor. At his passing, the eulogies that went up over India were not to John Hyde, Presbyterian missionary from Streeter, Illinois. Rather, the people praised Praying Hyde, the name India knew and loved him for. He had moved that nation toward God and had seen multitudes won to Christ through his fervent prayer ministry. Prayer for spiritual awakening can do that.

This principle not only works on an individual basis; it also has a corporate aspect. A man of God in early America, Nathaniel Emmons, believed that fervent prayer for the advancement of the kingdom of God and for the growth of the church was the responsibility of every believer. He declared: "Our Savior taught His disciples to pray for the future enlargement of His Kingdom saying, 'Thy Kingdom come, Thy will be done on earth as it is in heaven.' God intends to send the gospel to the ends of the earth and bring all nations into His

Kingdom. And we may presume that the fervent prayers of myriads of pious Christians, will avail much to bring about this great and desirable event. . . . Indeed, it is our indispensable duty to pray for the accomplishment of all the purpose and predictions of God, which remain to be accomplished."[6]

Many spiritual giants of the past and present understand this principle. The pioneer missionary William Carey stated: "If a temple is raised for God in the heathen world, it will not be by might, nor by power, nor by the authority of the magistrate, or the eloquence of the orator; but by my Spirit, saith the Lord of hosts. We must therefore be in real earnest in supplicating his blessings upon our labors."[7]

Timothy Dwight, man of God and president of Yale University at the turn of the nineteenth century, saw revival sweep that secular campus. So profound did the movement become that Yale was transformed into a citadel of revival. In a sermon entitled "Revivals of Religion," President Dwight emphasized the centrality and importance of labor and prayer for an awakening. Emphasizing the centrality of prayer, he stated, "It is not sufficient that you labor. If you would find success, you must pray also. No good descends from heaven to this world, except in answer to prayer."[8]

The great Prayer Revival of 1858 transformed not only America and the churches but the British Isles as well. In the two years that followed the outbreak of the Prayer Revival, according to historian Edwin Orr, fifty thousand new converts were added to the churches in America every month for two years. At that time there were only thirty million people in the United States. Translate that into contemporary population statistics, and it would mean between four hundred and five hundred thousand new converts added to our churches every month for two years. That is church growth. And it all came about by fervent prayer.

Only one conclusion can be drawn: Prayer and spiritual awakening and church growth go together. We know all these things. We have stressed it over and again. But why don't we do something about it in the light of these facts?

THE BURDEN OF PRAYER

The sum of the matter is that a *burden of prayer* must settle down on the people of God if we are to see revival. The challenge to intercession should be put before believers in preaching, teaching, writing, and every possible means. Yet, only the Holy Spirit can burden God's people for revival to stem the tide of secularism and godlessness. We would be wise to begin by praying for such a burden to come upon the church.

The Spirit of God makes clear to Christians that multitudes are rushing into eternity oblivious of the fact that they have not settled accounts with God. Surely this should burden God's people. The Spirit constantly moves his people to realize what God sees as life's priorities. Is it buildings, budgets, and programs that we often visualize as so important and to which we give ourselves and our resources? Are these the vital issues? These things certainly have an important place, but they play a secondary, supportive role. The church must be brought to the end of its self-seeking and come to understand what matters most in God's mission of kingdom advance: *People*. People need the Lord! And whatever it takes to reach them, to that the church should first give itself. Other concerns matter only as they support this central kingdom goal. The church does not exist for itself. The church exists for the glory of Jesus Christ, the advancement of his kingdom through bringing people to the foot of the cross, and forming Christ in God's people. Prayer for revival lays the foundation for this to happen. May we, therefore, make that "method" paramount.

God's people must, moreover, develop a burden and concern for righteousness to reign in society. Our Lord deserves to be vindicated. This is his world; he is the Creator and Sustainer. He must not be ignored or passed by. God reveals himself as the Almighty One, and he intends his righteousness and holiness to permeate every fabric of society as well as the church. When a burden like this settles in on the people of God, it drives them to prayer.

Furthermore, deep concern and commitment will bring about the purification of the church, and priorities will be kept in balance.

People in their desperate needs assume a central role, and the vindication of God's sovereign rule will be established. Then great honor and glory will be ascribed to the Lord. May God's people join together in the kind of praying that brings real revival and church growth that will extend into eternity.

All of this implies that the church needs to develop a vital prayer ministry. A clarion call for prayer is sweeping the Western world today. Parachurch organizations, denominational programming, and many individual leaders and laymen alike are calling God's people to their knees for revival. In the city where this author serves in theological education, an organization called "Birmingham Alive" fosters concern for prayer. Various denominations and churches have come together to inspire corporate prayer that God will "come alive" and pour out his Holy Spirit on our city and land. This kind of call demands several things of the church.

E. M. Bounds expressed it correctly when he said: "What the church needs today is not more machinery or better, not new organizations or more novel methods, but men whom the Holy Ghost can use—men of prayer, men mighty in prayer. The Holy Ghost does not flow through methods, but through men. He does not come on machinery, but on men. He does not anoint plants, but men—men of prayer."[9]

Without a mighty moving of the Holy Spirit, generated by prayer, all is in vain. Spurgeon declared, "If we have not the Spirit of God, let us write 'Ichabod' over our door and go home and pray until we have Him." Prayer brings the power of God.

All of these attestations to the centrality of God working through prayer implies that we must do more than inspire people to pray. We must also teach them the rudiments of prayer. Following are some revival prayer principles that need to be fused into the people of God.

THE RUDIMENTS OF PRAYER: INTERCESSION

Great prayer principles can be found in the well-known intercession of Solomon at the dedication of the Jewish temple in Jerusalem.

Solomon prayed and God answered: "If . . . My people who are called by My name humble themselves and pray, and seek My face and turn from their wicked ways, then I will hear from heaven, will forgive their sin, and will heal their land" (2 Chron. 7:13–14). Notice the salient points of this pungent prayer. First, God's people, "called by His name," are the ones whom God challenges to be humble, praying people. We stand before God as his redeemed people, recipients of his undeserved grace. In gratitude for our position in Christ, we humble ourselves and pray. A genuine spirit of humility should permeate our prayer as we come to recognize our dependence upon God and his gracious, undeserved favor.

Then we must learn to prevail in prayer. We must "seek God's face" until he looks on us and sends revival. Unless a praying remnant prevails, there will be no revival. The key word is *prevail.* Society's precarious position should force us to prevailing prayer. Our spiritual condition is serious indeed.

In his classic volume, *The Rise and Fall of the Roman Empire,* author Edward Gibbon laid out the dynamics that brought the downfall of the mighty Roman Empire. Every destructive element in Rome that he set forth in his classic work now runs rampant in Western society. When we say we will have "revival or perish," we are not parroting a cliché. We need to see the face of God.

Then, we must "turn from our own wicked ways." When Isaiah saw the "Lord . . . high and lifted up" (Isa. 6:1 KJV), he cried out, "Woe is me" (v. 5). He saw himself as undone, ruined, because of his own personal sin. And he was specific about that sin. He had "unclean lips" (v. 5). We all have our individual sins that must be dealt with specifically if our prayer hopes to ascend before holy God in Christ.

When we prevail and call incessantly, then we have the promise that God will "hear from heaven, forgive our sins, and heal our land." Our land desperately needs to be healed. We could fall like Rome. How important it is that God's people come together, be taught the rudiments of prayer, and be encouraged to pray without ceasing for revival.

Of course, we must pray individually as well. Remember the tremendous experience of Jacob in his encounter with God? That became a transferring, reviving experience for the patriarch.

JACOB'S PRAYER

Our choice inevitably becomes that which Jacob faced during his return from Haran on his way to his father Isaac. He had an encounter that forced him to decide if he were going to serve God on a "human" or on a "divine" level. In that sense the decision for us revolves around whether we will be a "Jacob" or an "Israel." The story is recorded in Genesis 32. Prayer was the crux of the matter.

Jacob still had some distance to travel to reach his father's home. He had been away many years. He had amassed a fortune and had built his own kingdom with flocks, children, and wives. He was a good personal kingdom builder. Even before leaving home he had connived to take away the birthright and blessing from his twin brother Esau. These incidents had forced him to flee to Haran in the first place. Esau vowed to kill him over the matter. Jacob excelled as a master manipulator. His name "Jacob" means "a crafty one." He was rightly named. He did believe in God; he had his "Bethel experience." Nevertheless, much of Jacob's experience seemed very humanistic—as his name implies.

Now the crunch had come. A scouting servant galloped into camp with shattering news. He cried to Jacob, "Your brother, Esau, is riding hard this way with four hundred armed men." Jacob almost collapsed with fear. He could visualize four hundred wild, revengeful Arabs riding like fury toward his camp. "Oh, why did I ever cheat my brother out of the birthright and blessing," Jacob moaned. But then "Jacob," the "crafty one," took over. *Now let me plan a crafty way to placate my brother,* he thought. He arranged three sets of gifts and sent them ahead to Esau. Then he divided his family into lots and sent them on. Jacob reasoned that perhaps by the time Esau's wild band got through the gifts and saw the family, he would be softened. He was living up to his name again. But would it work? Jacob trembled. Then he prayed: "Oh, God, help, help. I'm not worthy, but help" (Gen. 32:9–12). He did have a measure of faith—but a small measure. But now Jacob had reached the end of "Jacob." The Scriptures tell us that he sent his wives and children over the Jabbok brook and alone came to grips with himself—and God.

On the other side of the brook, the Bible says Jacob met *a man*. But he was not a "man" at all. God wrestled with Jacob that night.

"Let me go," cried the man.

"No," cried Jacob. "Not until you bless me."

"Let me go!"

"No."

"Let me go!"

"No, I will not let you go unless you bless me," cried the anguished Jacob.

"If you do not let me go," cried the man, "I will smite you and you will limp through life."

"Then smite me. I'll be a cripple but I will not let you go until you bless me." Jacob hung on. God struck him, and for the rest of his life he did limp. The struggle went on for hours. Finally the man asked, "What is your name?" Of course, God *knew* his name, but he wanted Jacob to *understand* it.

"My name is Jacob; the 'supplanter,' 'the crafty one,'" Jacob acknowledged. "Yes, that's my name, and that's what I am."

"No," said God. "You are no longer Jacob; you are now *Israel*—one who wrestles and prevails with God. A kingdom of power is yours. The blessing and birthright are yours, Israel. *You have prevailed.*"

The drama closes as the rising sun sheds its first rays over the eastern horizon. Silhouetted on the top of a sand dune, Israel and his brother Esau embraced in reconciliation. Prayer truly changes things.

What will it be for us in our quest for a spiritual awakening? Will we be a "Jacob," using our skills and craftiness in a human fashion? Or will we be an "Israel," one who prevails with God. Revival victory grows out of wrestling with God—wrestling in fervent prayer. Heavenly power lies here and here alone. We may limp through life, but we will prevail. People may not understand, but we will prevail. We may not do as we once did, but we will prevail. Jacob or Israel? Which will it be? God reveals himself in reviving power and "hears from heaven" only through *Israelites!*

CORPORATE PRAYER

Person to person, we can meet God and prevail. God desires every individual believer to pray and to pray earnestly. But prayer undertaken on a corporate level holds an important place in revival. Many avenues can be explored and attempted in developing plans for corporate prayer. The church that develops an ongoing, broad-based, multifaceted prayer ministry creates the best church growth program possible.

A dynamic corporate prayer ministry should be developed to the point that no church member would be able to say, "There is no way that I can engage in the church's prayer ministry." If the program is broad-based and comprehensive, there should be some aspect of the prayer ministry in which everyone can engage. Here are a few suggestions.

1. Prayer breakfasts, especially for men, have proved helpful. Often they can be coupled with Bible study. Or it could be a prayer luncheon. The Prayer Revival of 1858 fits this pattern perfectly. It began when Jeremiah Lamphier, a lay missionary working with the Dutch Reformed Church on Fulton Street, New York City, asked businessmen to devote their lunch hour to prayer in the consistory building. Only six men attended the first session, and they came almost half an hour late. But they had a good prayer time and decided to carry on the next week. When the next prayer group assembled, sixteen businessmen gathered. They prayed through the hour. It became the fuse that set off an explosion that sent shock waves of prayer power throughout the entire land. It all began with a small group of men meeting for prayer at a specific time. Any church can devise this sort of approach.

2. Women can also be brought together for prayer teas or the like. In the Hebrides Revival of 1949, two elderly sisters met and interceded faithfully in prayer. Women have been wonderfully used in prayer through God's dealing with his people. Hannah interceded fer-

vently for a son, and the prophet Samuel was born. The biblical and historic illustrations are endless. Evelyn Christenson, in her classic book, *What Happens When Women Pray*, has called women to prayer. She wrote: "I . . . learned the simple process of envisioning my God when approaching Him in prayer. The joy that floods my whole being as I find myself visualizing all God is—all His love, all His power, all His concern for me—defies description. What greater privilege could there be for a human being than to actually *draw nigh* to the omnipotent, omniscient God, high and lifted up on His throne in glory? This to me is the most precious part of my prayer time."[10]

Any church can design a plan that features women gathering together in small groups for the purpose of praying for revival. The Spirit will lead.

3. Prayer partners can be instituted. Perhaps this can be done on the job, or in homes, or at any convenient venue. It can even be done on the telephone. Such an exercise brings camaraderie in the Spirit. It has often been used by God to precipitate a profound moving of the Holy Spirit.

4. Prayer chains can be devised. Many congregations have a prayer calendar that goes on twenty-four hours a day, seven days a week. It takes a church of some size to fill all the hours, but churches can at least move in a limited fashion in this direction. People can be urged to sign up for a specific period of time on a regular basis—perhaps to come to the church building—and give themselves to prayer. This has been very effective in many congregations. A case in point is the great Second Baptist Church of Houston, Texas. The prayer ministry of this congregation is a beautiful testimony to what a church chain of prayer can accomplish. The Houston church has become one of the most rapidly growing, ministering churches in the United States. Much of their success is due to the fervent prayers of the people.

5. Another approach consists of all-night chains of prayer. A dedicated layman and this author planted a new church in Fort Worth, Texas. We got off to a good start, and God blessed the work in a gracious manner. One day one of the members of the little congregation

came to me as his pastor and suggested that we have an all-night chain of prayer every Saturday night. We were small in number, and we questioned whether enough people would commit themselves for a specific hour, especially through the night. But God's people responded when the challenge was put before them. The Lord had been working among us in a wonderful way, and the folks had a hunger and willingness to see God do great things.

The prayer ministry got underway. For the next year, I can honestly say that I had never seen such a continual moving of the Holy Spirit in my ministry. It brought God's presence and power among us. Some of the wonderful blessings that emerged out of that simple prayer plan proved marvelous indeed. People came to faith in the Lord Jesus Christ. Such a surge of spiritual growth took place among God's people that it was a blessing to behold. God dwelt with us in a beautiful manner. Again, it came about through prayer.

There are many different approaches to engaging people in prayer. All-day seasons of prayer can be held with the people gathering together in the church from 8:00 Saturday morning to 8:00 Saturday night to intercede. (It can be done throughout the entire night as well.) I was once in a church that did this during an evangelistic series. We fasted and prayed. As a result, we had one of the greatest evangelistic ingathering that I had ever been involved in. Many means can be devised by innovative, thoughtful, and earnest church leaders.

FASTING AND PRAYER

Does fasting have a place in the ministry of prayer? In the life and ministry of our Lord, an interesting encounter with the Pharisees occurred. Luke recorded it in his Gospel: "And they said to Him, 'The disciples of John often fast and offer prayers; the disciples of the Pharisees also do the same; but Yours eat and drink.' And Jesus said to them, 'You cannot make the attendants of the bridegroom fast while the bridegroom is with them, can you? But the days will come; and when the bridegroom is taken away from them, then they will fast in those days'" (5:33–35).

Our Lord intends his people, at least on occasion, to fast as well as pray. There are various approaches to this discipline. For example, one such program suggests a forty-day prayer fast. This has become a popular exercise in recent years. This does not mean no food or water but a giving up of certain aspects of the physical needs of the body in order to give oneself more to prayer. As the burden deepens, fasting becomes a natural outcome of a deep burden. One must be open to how the Spirit of God leads in these matters. Prayer coupled with fasting can be a helpful exercise. But we should guard against legalism and pride in this matter.

CONCLUSION

Why do some churches fail to grow? Leonard Ravenhill answered the question when he said, "The church is dead on its feet because it is not alive on its knees." But when God's people do get "on their knees," vitality and growth result. So the issue again is, what will we do about it? Do we really want our church to grow on a kingdom basis? Do we long to see genuine conversions and God's people deepened and moved into a life of devoted discipleship? If we give an affirmative answer to these questions, we must develop prayer. This calls for sacrifice. But as E. Stanley Jones said, "The future of the world may well be determined by small groups of people praying, thinking and acting beyond the rest."[11] The sacrifice is worth it. May God grant us grace in our churches and in our individual lives to throw ourselves into this vital discipline. Prayer brings God; God brings revival; revival brings growth. This is the divine formula for greatness.

TEN QUESTIONS FOR STUDY

1. What was the secret of Spurgeon's effective ministry? Does this have anything to say to us today?

2. Discuss the centrality of prayer throughout the history of the church.

3. How does the burden for prayer come about?

4. What do we mean by *intercession?*

5. What must be dealt with to make prayer heard by God?

6. What is the meaning of *prevailing* in prayer?

7. How is the church to pray as a body? How does this relate to revival and growth?

8. What are some of the "programs" of prayer that a church can institute?

9. How does fasting relate to prayer?

10. What are you going to do about your prayer life?

CHAPTER 10

USER-FRIENDLY WORSHIP IN SPIRITUAL AWAKENING AND CHURCH GROWTH

Churches struggle today with the revolution in worship style. Many dynamics have created the situations: The Boomer generation has a taste for different music; the charismatic movement asserts itself; the return of some of Generation X-Bridger to the traditional worship of the Greek Orthodox Church—all these have exerted an influence. These and many other dynamics have put more than one church in a quandary about how they should structure their worship services. The existential postmodern age in which we live makes this problem even more acute.

At the same time, however, it is possible that new worship experiences will revitalize congregations. Revival has usually precipitated new worship styles. As a consequence, the unbelieving community often comes alive to the new vitality of the church in worship. But this issue has also caused internal conflict. The ultimate solution will most likely be found in the concept of worship as "user-friendly." But when we address the worship issue, what are we really talking about?

THE ESSENCE OF WORSHIP

Worship centers in the adoration of God. But meaningful worship is experienced only when we understand the God whom we are attempting to extol in our worship experiences. Therefore, when the church enters into worship, it needs a clear grasp of the greatness of God. As the psalmist expressed it, "For Thou art great and doest wondrous deeds; Thou alone art God" (Ps. 86:10). Who is this great God whom we worship, and what does he wondrously do? This question thrusts us back into the discussion in an earlier chapter on the significant "omni" expressions of God. He is omnipotent (all-powerful), omniscient (all knowing), and omnipresent (at all places at all times). God stands absolutely and fully transcendent, above and beyond his creation. Even the terms that describe God with the prefix "omni" fall short of his glory. Therefore, to express God's full personhood with our limited human language is impossible. Beyond that, we know him to be consuming holiness. This attribute results in a standard of righteousness, morality, and ethical principles wherein we fall pitifully short.

Yet, we have also learned that this great God abounds in grace, mercy, and love. He reaches out to us in long-suffering patience and inexhaustible compassion. Thus, through Jesus Christ, he cleanses, saves, restores, redeems, and makes us into a new people who are acceptable in his sight. This, as far as we can understand, is the great God whom we extol in our worship as we lift up into his presence the adoration and gratitude of our hearts. Little wonder the Book of Psalms ends with these words: "Praise the LORD! Praise God in His sanctuary; praise Him in His mighty expanse. Praise Him for His mighty deeds; praise Him according to His excellent greatness. . . . Let everything that has breath praise the LORD. Praise the LORD!" (150:1–2, 6). With the totality of our being, we extol the God who is our Creator, Sustainer, and Redeemer. As inconceivable as it may seem, he is our loving, gracious heavenly Father. He loves us to the point of actually loving our sincere worship and praise. God's divine personhood creates the proper attitude and understanding for meaningful worship.

THE PROPER ATTITUDE IN WORSHIP

When the Spirit ushers us into the throne room of God's grace, and we cast eyes upon the beautiful One who sits on the throne, the overwhelming sense that besets us can only be described as *awe*. The Bible abounds in the expression "the *fear* of the Lord." The word *fear* literally means "awesomeness." When we get only a glimpse of our God, awe is the only reasonable spirit and attitude in which to address him. The hymn writer Charles H. Gabriel expressed it well: "I stand amazed in the presence of Jesus the Nazarene." Everything about our great God, his Son Jesus Christ, and the abiding Holy Spirit brings amazement, wonder, and awe to our hearts.

Moreover, this sense of awe strikes a spirit of deep humility within the heart. The second line of the hymn quoted above reads, "And wonder how he could love me, a sinner, condemned, unclean." When we see God, we inevitably see ourselves. Our human depravity looms large in the light of holy God. As related earlier, the classic case is the prophet Isaiah (6:1–12). When Moses saw the Lord, he also cried, "I AM FULL OF FEAR and trembling" (Heb. 12:21b). This reality should bring us to honesty and the humility befitting us as sinful creatures. Yet, wonder of wonders, he accepts us in Jesus Christ. Therefore, we can stand in his glorious presence, even stand boldly (4:16). In Christ we can glory in the final line of the hymn writer's exaltation, "How marvelous, how wonderful is my Savior's love for me."

Awe, humility, and faith lay the basic attitude stones as we raise the structure of true worship of God. Worship develops a spirit of deep, profound gratitude for his person, his greatness and glory, and his amazing grace. Thanksgiving and gratitude well up within us, and we praise the Lord. When spiritual awakenings occur, the church of Jesus Christ worships as never before.

THE FRUIT OF WORSHIP

Real worship immediately leads us to surrender to God's sovereign will. This is the primary fruit of worship. When God revealed himself and the challenge to mission came to the prophet Isaiah, he said: "Here am I. Send me!" (Isa. 6:8). In those five pungent words, Isaiah surrendered to the great God whom he was worshiping. Rebellion and worship stand in total opposition to each other. A hardened heart and a seared conscience with a verbal praise of God are so incongruous that it borders on blasphemy. The true worshiping soul becomes the surrendered soul.

Worship finally culminates in selfless, abandoned adoration. God is worthy to be adored—adored for who he is, for what he has done and is doing and the bright future he has designed for all of his creation. Adoration and praise belong to our God. In this spirit of adoring worship, we are blessed with new life, vitality, redirection, cleansing, spiritual power, and reality. Worship is life and power.

THE POWER AND INSIGHTS OF WORSHIP

Worship is a rich source of incredible spiritual power. Look briefly at some of the blessings that emanate from sincere, knowledgeable worship of God. First, God smiles on our worship. The fact that he is pleased and that he approves our worship—actually seeks it—is a rich blessing to our open hearts. It boggles the mind that God in his holy personhood looks down upon us in our finitude and approves us with words like these: "Well done, good and faithful servant. Your praise is accepted." But it is true. God desires and actually enjoys our worship.

Second, sincere worship unfolds in *Spirit,* the Holy Spirit, and in *truth* (John 4:24). This means worship in honesty and truth come through the inspiration, direction, and empowerment of God's Spirit. Our Lord stands as the "outside" object of worship. But by his indwelling Holy Spirit he works within us to make our worship dynamic, life-changing, and Christ honoring. This level of worship does not arise because of the beauty of our temples or from the form of worship—whether liturgical or unstructured. What makes worship true worship is God's activity as he directs, inspires, and breathes reality into our hearts and minds.

Furthermore, we worship in Spirit and in *truth.* This involves honesty, sincerity, and a grasp of God's truth concerning himself. The truth of God, as he reveals himself in the context of worship, becomes a vital element. Worship is not all emotion. An objective element of truth resides at the core of genuine worship. The truth of God as revealed in the Word of God becomes the standard by which we understand God's nature, what pleases him, and how to worship him properly. It also implies mental and spiritual discipline. We do not always "feel" like worshiping. But we do so regardless. We know and understand who he is when we worship and that he deserves our praise regardless of our feelings. Then we intelligently give him the adoration of our hearts in Jesus' name, and our worship becomes acceptable.

Truth in worship lasts not for the short term, but for life. Worship actually becomes a lifestyle (Rom. 12:1–2). This is why true worship becomes attractive to the unbelieving world. Many people have come to faith in Christ in the context of the church in living worship.

Worship also brings conviction into the experience of believers. The Book of Psalms, which is almost a textbook on worship, uses expressions like: "Search me, O God, and know my heart" (139:23). When we come into the presence of God, we often find some area of life that needs to be brought under the blood of Christ and submitted to his lordship. Worship leads to new steps in our quest for godliness and holiness.

In a word, worship becomes a dynamic exercise. God is as the source of all reality. He alone can bring meaning to the human experience. Thus, real worship becomes a powerful, life-changing experience. It brings renewal to the people of God and salvation to those who need Jesus Christ. Genuine worship can even help spawn revival. The more God is worshiped and adored, the more we as humans see ourselves in the light of his personhood. We fall at his feet in humble submission and praise. Worship is a power for growth and kingdom progress.

TODAY'S CONFLICT IN WORSHIP

If worship serves all these constructive purposes, why the problem with style today? This issue should dissipate in genuine worship. Whether we clap our hands, stand or sit, use a hymnbook or a projection screen, true worship emanates from the heart. Why then do we still experience so many problems with contemporary worship? But then again, our current state of confusion is nothing new. There have been so-called "revolutions" in worship many times.

When Isaac Watts came on the scene in the eighteenth century and began to write the great hymns that we now call "traditional," he became a radical innovator. A world of difference exists between Isaac Watts's hymns and the Gregorian chants of the Middle Ages. Isaac Watts set his beautiful poems to the music sung in the pubs of England, as did Martin Luther in Germany. Some contemporaries of Watts and Luther thought it too revolutionary. To others it was even scandalous. Still, others responded to it positively because it was the kind of music they understood.

These revolutions in worship styles have been going on for centuries. The fact that we find ourselves in one at the moment should not startle us. True, a real difference exists between the hymnody of the nineteenth century, epitomized in writers like Fanny Crosby, and what we hear today. The new generation has been brought up on rock and roll, country music, and the like; the older generation likes ballads and the "big bands." Music, a communicative medium in worship, is bringing about the radical shift in our hymnody.

NEW STYLE

At the same time, the new paradigm emerging in church music has filtered down into other aspects of Christian worship. Clerical dress, robed choirs, liturgical forms, and many other traditions surrounding traditional worship seem to be fading away, especially in the postmodern mind-set of the younger generations. Even coats and ties for men and more formal dresses for women are out. For many, "Sunday dress" is passé. This is not easy for the older generation to understand, let alone accept. The problem of worship probably grows out of the paradigm shift in the communication and lifestyle of today. The older generation did not grow up with television, computers, and guitars. The younger generation does not understand the communicative and cultural style of their elders. So the conflict goes on.

Few would disagree with the idea that we must create a user-friendly worship style—a style where people feel comfortable and where they can feel somewhat "at home." Worship should always be done in such a manner that people may be able to understand, assimilate, and act upon the experience that genuine worship conveys. To insist upon ways of doing things and using communicative styles that are not alive and "friendly" can be a mistake. If we want people to have a genuine worship experience and truly meet God, we must give worship a stylistic relevance that addresses contemporary society in its need. As church growth leader Thom Rainer has said, "American missionaries to foreign mission fields have long recognized the need to contextualize, or to adapt culturally to their mission field. American churchgoers must realize that our nation is culturally diverse, and new churches are needed to offer worship services in the cultures that are being reached."[1] This demands maturity and acceptance on all sides.

THE NEED

Worship in today's context requires a measure of spiritual maturity. We must recognize that we do not come together in worship primarily to get ourselves satisfied. We worship God for his glory. This means that the younger generation needs to be willing to accept some of the more traditional elements of worship. On the other hand, the traditionalists need to be open to the free style of the moderns. Remember, the God whom we worship is immutable; he never changes. Our styles of worship are secondary—important, but secondary. It's easy to get too involved in *how* we worship and forget *whom* we worship.

An interesting incident in this regard occurred in the divinity school where this author teaches. The leader of our chapel worship services had a student to say to him, "If we sing any more hymns out of the traditional hymnbook, I'm not coming to chapel anymore." The worship leader replied, "I had a student in here two days ago who said, 'If we don't start using the hymnbook and stop using that projection screen, I'm not coming to chapel services any longer!'" Both attitudes were not very mature. Church members must come to an acceptance and an appreciation of different worship styles. The mature worshiper should be able to adapt to different ways of worship. How can this be worked out in peace and harmony?

MAKING PEACE

Churches have used various approaches to try to resolve the conflict in worship. Of course, when new churches are planted, they usually are more "contemporary" in their approach from the very beginning. They experience little conflict, although this may mean a certain element in some communities will remain unreached. But most established churches still struggle with the problem, trying to find some way to make peace and still be user-friendly. Is there an answer to this dilemma? Some things that have taken place in some churches have proven helpful.

First, all churches need to realize that worship *is worship of God.* For example, whether or not we like the music is not the main point. Music is no more than a communication medium. But at the same time, we are wise to be communicative with our worship. True worship is "in spirit and in truth." Style is not the primary issue.

An approach being used today is the so-called "blended service." For example, choruses and praise songs as well as traditional hymns will be sung. From time to time a dramatic presentation may be given, but not necessarily on a regular basis. The special music will often be quite contemporary, but occasionally a traditional choir may sing a very traditional hymn or even an anthem. In the church where my wife and I worship, the organist played Bach's "Toccata and Fugue in D Minor" during one morning worship service. That night the same organist led the worship service in a contemporary way, accompanied by a saxophone. And the musicians received applause in both services. Someone has said that our worship services ought to have everything from "rock to Bach"—and we did that Sunday.

Some people may object to this approach, but it has an element of wisdom nonetheless. Blended services will often reach a broad spectrum of the community. No one may be absolutely satisfied, but a mature approach and the consideration of others can make a blended service quite effective.

Smaller churches in smaller communities must do something like the blended service. Of course, there are congregations that have committed themselves to a certain target group like the Boomers. This means they design the entire life of the church to reach them. In a large metropolitan area this may be acceptable because other churches can reach out to other generations. But in the smaller towns and communities where there are no other churches, the blended service seems the only option.

OTHER ISSUES

Many issues in creating user-friendly worship go beyond worship style alone. Many people today do not work the traditional eight daylight hours, Monday through Friday. Many shift workers and store clerks work at night and through the weekends. We should worship at the time and the place where we can be most user-friendly. Some churches are having Saturday night worship services, for example. And we do not have to worship at eleven o'clock in the morning to receive God's favor; any hour will do. We no longer live under the old covenant where the "Sabbath" must be kept at all costs. Jesus once and for all changed that. We have been thrust into the task of reaching people for worship and the praise of Christ; let us be wise in doing so.

Other churches have moved to multiple services, not necessarily because of space needs but in order to target certain elements in the community. The generation gaps in years past did not prove too significant. But how different things are today! Multiple services allow different styles. We must use appropriate approaches to reach the greatest number of people.

We live in a revolutionary time today, and we must make our worship services as alive and user-friendly as possible. This demands thought, prayer, experimentation, and tenacity until the church finds its proper niche in worship. Maturity on the part of the worshipers is essential. No one will like every aspect of any service. But we gather together to worship God—*not to be entertained.* The "entertainment syndrome" can be a real pitfall. Some churches have not been very sensitive at this point. True worship—regardless of style—encourages a genuine moving of the Spirit of God. This can be one of the vital factors of revival and church growth. We are going to spend eternity worshiping God; it will be wise to learn to do it here. But meaningful worship demands planning.

USER-FRIENDLY WORSHIP AND ITS PLANNING

Paul told the Corinthian church that everything should "be done properly and in an orderly manner" (1 Cor. 14:40). This should not be interpreted legalistically; a real place for freedom in worship exists. The Bible states, "Where the Spirit of the Lord is, there is liberty" (2 Cor. 3:17). At the same time, however, this does not mean we have license to create a free-for-all worship service with no rhyme or reason. Some worship today seems more like chaos than real worship. A genuine difference exists between liberty and license, even in worship. Paul reminds us, "God is not a God of confusion" (1 Cor. 14:33). This suggests a biblical pattern that our Lord approves.

In the Old Testament, the "solemn assembly" has a lesson to teach us. Worship is a solemn experience. This does not mean it has no joy or exuberance. To the contrary, Paul said we should be "speaking to one another in psalms and hymns and spiritual songs, singing and making melody with your heart to the Lord; always giving thanks for all things in the name of our Lord Jesus Christ to God, even the Father" (Eph. 5:19–20). The concept of "solemness" means a genuine spirit of awe in the presence of God, humility before our Maker, an awareness of our need, conviction of our sin, and the wonderful cleansing of the blood of Christ as we submit ourselves to him in deeper dedication. Biblical worship principles should always be infused into the context of worship. To plan our worship so that it gives God a chance to reveal himself and to speak to us is the wise procedure.

Because planning has a role in worship, input from various elements of the congregation should be integrated into good worship. One of the weaknesses in many churches today, especially more traditional churches, is that little planning goes into the worship experience. Yet we live in a day in which corporations will spend millions of dollars on just one thirty-second commercial on television. Today's TV-oriented people are accustomed to seeing things done concisely, pungently, and extremely well. If they come to our churches and experience slipshod, ill-planned worship, they will be bored if not turned off. Worship services should be alive and vibrant. They should move with a dynamic, pungent relevancy that captivates the worshiper. That constitutes the kind of communication that people receive today. To fail to recognize this is a serious error on the part of worship planners.

One person, even a well-trained pastor, is generally not capable of doing all the planning and strategizing of worship completely on his own. There should be at least a worship committee where input and evaluation from others can be included in the planning. If possible, the services should be taped. Then the services can be analyzed and evaluated on a week-by-week basis. All of this takes time and effort. But that time when the church gathers for worship presents a golden opportunity. More things for the glory of Christ take place during this time than probably any other given moment in the life of the church.

Worship does not begin and end with the music. The preaching of God's Word, the prayers—even the collection of the offering—are important parts of the worship experience. All should be seen in this light and planned and done well.

People come to worship essentially to experience God, whether they realize it or not. If the presence of God is genuinely encountered in worship, the style of worship fades into insignificance. When Isaiah saw the Lord, "high and lifted up" (Isa. 6:1 KJV), he did not question if the seraphim crossed their wings over their feet (v. 2) just the way he liked to see the heavenly beings do it. He stood face-to-face before God, and the experience consumed him. When a person meets God in worship, this is all that really matters.

CONCLUSION

Planning with an awareness of the modern cultural situation recognizes that the modern mentality is not only different; it changes rapidly. But we worship to meet God. Relevant communication is important in our Christian enterprise, certainly in worship. Thus, we are wise to get on the level of the people we wish to touch. The gospel never changes. Jesus and his truth remain the same yesterday, today, and forever. God does not change; he remains the same. But we must be faithful to our Lord in presenting his truth in a fashion that addresses people where they are and on the basis of their needs in a fashion that is attractive to them. When we do that, they come. The worship of God contributes significantly to church growth.

TEN QUESTIONS FOR STUDY

1. What is the role of worship among God's people?
2. Why do we worship God?
3. Is worship important?
4. Why the conflict in worship today?
5. What is worship anyway? What is the goal of the exercise?
6. Can solutions to the conflict over worship be found? Where? How?
7. How can a church train people in worship? Should we even try? Why or why not?
8. What is your church doing about the issue? Is it a good program? What needs surface today, if any?
9. What happens to worship when revival fire falls?
10. Does effective worship impact the unbelieving community and thus grow the church? Why? Give examples.

CHAPTER 11

THE "UNUSUAL" IN SPIRITUAL AWAKENING AND CHURCH GROWTH

When the Second Great Awakening arrived on the American scene, the dramatic turn of events startled the multitudes. One of the most unusual aspects of the movement consisted of the manifestations that took place. This proved particularly true on the emerging frontier. Although the thrust had its early harbingers in the eastern states, as the western expansion exploded with pioneers, the multitudes moving west were caught up in the new spirit. A profound revival swept the land.

THE SECOND GREAT AWAKENING

The First Great Awakening had its beginnings among New England Congregationalists and Presbyterians. The Second Great Awakening broke out primarily among Methodists and Baptists. Although it was largely a Baptist and Methodist movement, the Presbyterians and others were not exempt. Impacted by the awakening were two North Carolina Presbyterian ministers, James McGready and Barton Stone. God destined McGready and Stone to be greatly used by the Holy Spirit in the revival. Trekking through the Cumberland Gap, they soon took up their ministries in Kentucky. James McGready, after two or three years in Tennessee, settled in Logan County, Kentucky, and began preaching at the Red River Meeting House.

Everyone saw McGready as an "impassioned preacher, diligent pastor, and fervent man of prayer."[1] In June of 1800 he challenged the people of south central Kentucky to gather for an extended four-day meeting—Friday through Monday. Sensing God's moving, many people arrived at Red River in expectation of blessings. They were not disappointed; the Holy Spirit fell in fantastic fashion. The first two days brought floods of repentant tears. The Spirit moved even deeper on Sunday as the Lord's Supper was served. The acme of the protracted meeting came when John McGee, a Methodist minister, preached the closing sermon. He described the scene: "I . . . exhorted them to let the Lord omnipotent reign in their hearts, and submit to him, and their souls should live. . . . I turned again and losing sight of fear of man, I went through the house shouting and exhorting with all possible ecstasy and energy, and the floor was soon covered by the slain."[2]

Some six thousand hungry-hearted people had come from a one-hundred-mile radius around Red River. No buildings to house the masses existed in the little country community, so they rolled out their tents, and some slept in their wagons. Thus the first camp meeting was born, all unplanned. But a new movement and methodology came into being. The experience overwhelmed the people. Unusual things occurred. Pastor McGready tells us: "No person seemed to wish to go home—hunger and sleep seemed to affect nobody—eternal things were the vast concern. Here awakening and converting work was to be found in every part of the multitude. . . . Sober professors, who had been communicants for many years, now lying prostrate on the ground, crying out in such language as this: 'O! How I would have despised any person a few days ago, who would have acted as I am doing now! But I cannot help it!' . . . persons of every description, white and black, were to be found in every part of the multitude . . . crying out for mercy in the most extreme distress."[3]

THE CANE RIDGE REVIVAL

Of the people who attended, God singled out for usefulness Barton Stone, McGready's young "Timothy." He had been preaching at the Cane Ridge Meeting House in Bourbon County, Kentucky, and had been urged to serve there by frontiersman Daniel Boone. Stone, deeply impressed with the Red River revival, went home and in May of 1801 called for a similar meeting at Cane Ridge. The work had begun. He scheduled another such meeting in August. To the astonishment of all, over twenty thousand people arrived for the six-day camp meeting; and this was the sparsely populated frontier.

Thousands were converted, among them James B. Finley. He later became a Methodist circuit rider. He described the Cane Ridge meeting:

The noise was like the roar of Niagara. The vast sea of human beings seemed to be agitated as if by a storm. I counted seven ministers, all preaching at one time, some on stumps, others in wagons, and one was standing on a tree which had, in falling, lodged against another. . . . Some of the people were singing, others praying, some crying for mercy in the most piteous accents, while others were shouting most vociferously. While witnessing these scenes, a peculiarly strange sensation, such as I had never felt before, came over me. My heart beat tumultuously, my knees trembled, my lips quivered, and I felt as though I must fall to the ground. A strange supernatural power seemed to pervade the entire mass of mind there collected. . . . I stepped up on to a log, where I could have a better view of the surging mass of humanity. The scene that then presented itself to my mind was indescribable. At one time I saw at least five hundred swept down in a moment, as if a batter of a thousand guns had been opened upon them and then immediately followed shrieks and shouts that rent the very heavens.[4]

The American frontier experienced a radical transformation. The "Bible Belt" of America's southeast was created. Revivalism, which continues to this day, had its birth in the movement. The camp meeting motif of evangelism spread all over eastern America. As the pioneers pushed Westward, Christian values characterized the early expansion of the west. God's great hour had come.

As so often happens, the frontier revival waned, just like the First Great Awakening. A subtle spiritual stagnation began to settle in. Charles Finney exercised a powerful ministry, but even he saw decline by 1840. But God was not through with the United States.

THE GREAT CENTURY

The churches of America experienced another profound awakening in the great Prayer Revival of 1858. This movement launched the widespread evangelistic ministry of D. L. Moody. Europe had its counterpart movement too. Little wonder the nineteenth century became known in church history circles as "The Great Century."

In all such movements, however, spiritual declension inevitably creeps in, seemingly cutting down the blessed results of the revival. Except for a few isolated places—such as Wheaton College in Illinois and Asbury College in Kentucky—in the last half of the twentieth-century, American Christianity has witnessed very few deep movements of the Holy Spirit. A flourish of interest developed after World War II during the late forties and fifties, but this faded during the revolutionary sixties and seventies.

TODAY'S POSSIBILITIES

Is there any hope today as the new millennium is ushered in? Are there any harbingers of an awakening on the immediate horizon? The answer is a guarded *yes*. America—and other parts of the world—could possibly be on the verge of another great awakening. This appears true for several reasons. First, God has periodically revived his work. He will not keep silent forever. Second, significant contemporary movements fostering revival concern seem to be rising. Moreover, and of most importance, prayer for spiritual awakening has become a burden for many people. It can happen again! If God in his sovereignty sees fit to declare, "This is the hour," these factors of concern and prayer can be interpreted in a positive light. If revival does come, we can expect unusual occurrences. Though all great awakenings have many traditional dynamics, unusual manifestations normally arise as well.

MANIFESTATIONS

These unusual manifestations have often caused an uproar in some circles. Take as a case in point the unusual phenomena that occurred during the Second Great Awakening. The occurrences were dubbed "exercises." For example, the so-called "running exercise" erupted. At Cane Ridge, people under the conviction of the Holy Spirit would run across the compound into the open fields. Others simply passed out under conviction of their sin and the impending judgment of God. Many who came to faith in Christ became so joyous that they would jump up and down and dance. There were even "jerks" and "groans" among some of the people.

A little less unusual were Finney's "new measures" during these revival times. They do not seem revolutionary to us today, but they certainly were in the first half of the nineteenth century. Finney popularized what finally evolved into the so-called "public invitation." Picking up the idea from the mourner's bench or the anxious seat, the evangelist would invite people to "come forward" in the meeting if they were "anxious" about their soul's salvation and would be willing to "mourn" over their sins. In that setting the modern evangelistic method of the invitation had its birth. Finney would also pray openly for lost people by name. He also held regular, organized meetings over a protracted period. Although this approach occurred to a limited extent in the First Great Awakening, it was not developed into an actual program until Finney came on the scene in the Second Great Awakening. The New York evangelist even allowed women to play a role in the work. He gave them the opportunity to pray aloud in congregations. That was really revolutionary in the early Victorian era.

These "new measures" precipitated not only serious debate but also a pastoral conference at New Lebanon, New York, to investigate the situation. Finney was grilled for days by the traditional ministers of

New England. Finney won, and the unusual became the usual. In that context modern mass evangelism had its beginning.

EXAMPLES

There has never been a great spiritual awakening without unusual manifestations. It was true in the biblical era. The Old Testament prophets, for example, used what has become known as "prophetic symbolism." Some of these prophets did unusual things to illustrate their message. God commissioned Moses through the unusual call of the burning bush. Moses then stood before Pharaoh, and ten miraculous occurrences took place. It broke Pharaoh's stubborn will. He finally released the Israelites that they might ultimately possess the Promised Land.

A dramatic story of the unusual took place in the contest between Elijah and the four hundred prophets of Baal on Mount Carmel. God's prophet called down fire from heaven. The Israelites were so struck by the awesomeness of the unusual occurrence that they cried out, "The LORD, He is God; the LORD, He is God" (1 Kings 18:39). And then there were miracles like the cleansing of Naaman's leprosy (2 Kings 5:1–14) and the raising of the Shunamite's son from the dead by Elisha (2 Kings 4:18–37).

In the New Testament era, it must have seemed unusual that a man, not formally educated, from a very insignificant village in Galilee, could go about healing. He placed his hands on blind people and they would see. He straightened crooked limbs, unstopped deaf ears, exorcised demons, walked on the water, and literally raised the dead. That was unusual, if not revolutionary. His name was Jesus.

The early church also experienced the unusual. The day of Pentecost dumbfounded the city of Jerusalem. Beginning from that event, the church fanned out over the Roman world sharing Christ, and unusual "signs and wonders" followed. The expression "signs and wonders" appears on page after page of the Acts of the Apostles. Those days were unusual times.

IT HAPPENS NOW

The same has been proven true of great spiritual stirrings among the people of God down through history. To restrict signs and wonders, miracles, and the "unusual" to the biblical era alone is a mistake. God has often worked in unusual ways in many parts of the world through the centuries. Multiplied manifestations of God's unusual power on countless fields can be recorded.

In 1927 a beautiful story emerged out of the Shantung Revival in northeast China. Baptist missionary Bertha Smith became one of the significant personalities in that powerful revival movement. In her classic work *Go Home and Tell,* she tells the story of how God did a most unusual thing that helped launch the Great Awakening. Her missionary colleagues gathered in a room to pray for the healing of the eyes of a fellow missionary, Mrs. Ola Culpepper. Ola suffered from optic neuritis, a very painful disease. Then it happened. But let Miss Bertha tell it in her own words:

I had gone into that room, so far as I knew, absolutely right with the Lord. I would not have dared to go otherwise. But when I stretched my hand out to Mrs. Culpepper's head, I had to bring it back. There stood facing me a missionary (Anna Hartwell) with whom there had been a little trouble. In her early years she had been head of a girls' school, but for several years she had been teaching illiterate women to read.

I had been asked to serve as principal in our boys' school in Chefoo while the missionary principal was on furlough. I had majored in education, and by that time had had ten years' experience in teaching and thought that I was "the last word" in education! I had recommended Miss Hartwell to lead daily worship in that school. After a few weeks, I asked another missionary to tell her that methods for teaching old women were not appropriate for high school boys. She was hurt, of course.

But what about my proud self? I did not have a particle of sympathy for her. Right there before everyone, I had to say,

"Miss Hartwell, I did not have the proper attitude toward you about that school affair. I beg you to forgive me!" My hand then joined the others and we prayed.

Had I refused to confess that sin, and joined in the prayer with it not covered, I believe that I would have hindered the prayer of the others, and the eye could not have been healed.

Because all were right with God and of one heart, heaven came down! We did not have to wait to see whether or not Mrs. Culpepper's eye was healed! We knew in our hearts that she would never have another attack. The Lord had heard the prayers of such human frailty and had performed a miracle in healing one whom we so loved! She did not put her glasses back on. While the sight was not restored completely in the weak eye, both were strengthened and not once has she had any more pain, though using her eyes steadily for reading and needlework.

Walking around the room rejoicing and praising the Lord, we were all on a mountaintop of ecstasy. Then I had to be the joy-killer. There came over me such a sense of our inconsistency that I had to speak of it.

"What kind of missionaries are we?" I asked. "We have gone through a week of heart-searching, humbling ourselves before each other and before the Lord, in order that we might be altogether right with him, so that he could hear our prayers and heal the physical eye of one of our own number. Yet we have never gone to this much self-negation for preparation to pray for the opening of the spiritual eyes of the Chinese to whom we have been sent." Our mountaintop of ecstasy suddenly became a valley of humiliation. We all went to our knees in contrite confession for having been so careless as to have gone along supposing that we were right with the Lord, while holding all kinds of attitudes which could have kept the Lord's living water from flowing through us to the Chinese.[5]

That's how the "unusual" figures in real revival. And unusual things still happen, right up to the present hour. The phenomenon holds an important place in revival.

SIGNS AND EVANGELISM

Manifestations of the Spirit present a strong testimony to Christ's presence and power. The promise of the Scripture stands as applicable for us today as when James first wrote it two thousand years ago. Recall his words: "Is anyone among you sick? Let him call for the elders of the church, and let them pray over him, anointing him with oil in the name of the Lord; and the prayer offered in faith will restore the one who is sick, and the Lord will raise him up, and if he has committed sins, they will be forgiven him. Therefore, confess your sins to one another, and pray for one another, so that you may be healed" (James 5:14–16).

Countless other acts of God's grace and power may occur in real revival. However, a serious word of caution is in order.

A WORD OF CAUTION

First, God never performs the unusual as an end in itself. He has great compassion and meets human needs, but John made clear in the fourth Gospel that God's unusual acts are miraculous *signs* of Christ's power and his divine personhood. They point to him—not to the event in itself—and they give our Lord authenticity. The ultimate purpose is to reveal to the world who Jesus is, to bring him glory, and to open the mind and heart of the skeptics as they cry out, "Nothing like this was ever seen in Israel" (Matt. 9:33). God *never* grants miracles for a superficial show or a shallow emotional high. Far more is involved in biblical "signs and wonders"; the wonders are *signs,* the point to Jesus.

The unusual often opens the hearts of those who are resistant to the gospel. When Paul suffered shipwreck on the Island of Crete, nothing was unusual about the event until a poisonous snake bit him and he did not drop dead. Then the apostle, by God's power, healed a leading citizen of the island. As a result, a great number believed, and a new church was planted. Things like this are the primary reasons for signs and wonders.

GOD MEETS NEEDS

God's unusual acts also meet the needs of hurting people. As the Spirit of God works in unusual ways through the various spiritual gifts with which he endows his people, untold good can be accomplished. Revival always reaches out to minister to all people in their multiplied hurts.

The salvation of people stands as the greatest sign and wonder that could possibly occur. This touches the deepest of all human needs. God reaches down into the depravity of human sin and snatches as a "brand plucked from the fire" (Zech. 3:2) those whom he will. This is miraculous beyond description. In this manner our unusual God does unusual things to build an unusual church to the unusual praise of Jesus. That helps make the field ripe for harvest.

Such signs also bring significant honor to Jesus Christ. Whenever something happens that does not bring praise to the Savior, it can be marked down as counterfeit. We must learn to "test the spirits," especially in our day. The final test of truth is the authentic truth that resides in Jesus Christ. That which is genuinely of the Spirit of God always exalts Jesus Christ and unfolds in the light of his divine personhood as revealed in the Scriptures.

WHAT TO AVOID

Errors and dangers must be scrupulously avoided. A biblical balance must be maintained. If a church gets unbalanced and carried away with the unusual, the results can be hurtful. We have made a case for the fact that unusual happenings can be completely and totally of God's Spirit. But it must be recognized that people can excite themselves and become too emotional. Counterfeit signs and wonders can occur. At times even Satan himself can slip in and perform the unusual to lead people away from the truth of Christ. The classic case in point involved the magicians in Egypt who counterfeited, apparently under satanic power, some of the miracles of Moses. Pharaoh hardened his heart and the entire nation suffered.

We must develop a sensitivity to the Spirit to make certain that the unusual emanates from his working and that it is not humanly generated—above all, that it is not demonic in nature. This is why John insisted, "Test the spirits to see whether they are from God" (1 John 4:1). Every aspect of church life must be tested by the Spirit and the Word of God. Error never grows a true church. We can easily give too much emphasis to the unusual. The Spirit of God often does his deepest, most profound work in a quiet, unobtrusive way. He does not always come in wind, earthquake, and fire, but sometimes in the "still small voice" (1 Kings 19:12 KJV). We must be careful in dealing with the phenomenal. Signs and wonders and unusual occurrences are not redemptive in themselves. Only the blood of Jesus Christ saves, and he alone is to be honored.

A danger even lurks in too much of an emphasis on the work of the Holy Spirit. A theologically unbalanced view of the Trinity can thus emerge. Jesus said, "He (the Holy Spirit) shall take of Mine, and shall disclose it to you" (John 16:14). Jesus and his glory always result from a genuine move of God's Spirit. People can even get caught up in excessive excitement and make shallow or false decisions for Christ. God wants his people balanced in theology and experience. Recall, Paul urged the Corinthian church to do all things "properly and in an orderly manner" (1 Cor. 14:40).

THE PRINCIPLES

Two basic principles must be kept in mind in order to gain a proper perspective to unusual occurrences during revival times. First, everything that takes place must be tested on the basis of the Scriptures. Of course, the Bible does not spell out in minute detail everything that may happen in the life of the church. But the Bible does present the principles with which to evaluate whether any movement is truly of God. Second, we should ask, What is the final fruit?

Jonathan Edwards was God's spokesman in America's First Great Awakening. Under his ministry there were many unusual signs. He struck a keynote when he acknowledged that religious affections can be legitimate: "It is evident, that religion consists so much in affection, as that without holy affection there is no true religion; and no light in the understanding is good, which does not produce holy affection in the heart; no habit or principle in the heart is good, which has no such exercise; and no external fruit is good, which does not proceed from such exercises."

But Edwards was also aware of the fact that Satan or the "flesh" can counterfeit religious affections:

> The subtlety of Satan . . . saw that affections were much in vogue, knowing the greater part of the land were not versed in such things, and had not had much experience of great religious affections to enable them to judge well of them, and distinguish between true and false; then he knew he could best play his game, by sowing tares amongst the wheat, and mingling false affections with the words of God's Spirit: he knew this to be a likely way to delude and eternally ruin many souls, and greatly to wound religion in the saints, and entangle them in a dreadful wilderness, and by and by, to bring all religion into disrepute.[6]

Affections generated by the Holy Spirit bring about unity, love, holiness, and godliness. These things are the true fruit of genuine unusual manifestations. So we must ask: Does the phenomenal meet biblical criteria, and is the consequence of any experience a life of Christlikeness? The issue is not the "show" but the shining forth of Jesus in a person's life. In a word, does the phenomenon exalt the Lord Jesus Christ and create holiness of life? If this criteria is met, we can conclude that the unusual can aid significant growth when properly used. May God grant us the wisdom to permit the Spirit of God to do as he wishes in furthering the kingdom of God. Then the local church will grow and manifest Jesus Christ in all of its life.

CONCLUSION

The unusual has its place in spawning spiritual awakening and bringing new life and vitality to the church. Signs and wonders can captivate the heart and mind of the unbelieving community as they bring glory to Jesus Christ. The result? The church will grow. We ought not close our minds to the unusual if we wish to see revival and subsequent growth of the church.

TEN QUESTIONS FOR STUDY

1. Are "unusual" happenings legitimate?
2. What does the Bible say about the "unusual"?
3. What does history say about the "unusual"?
4. Did miracles end in the first century?
5. What evidence of "signs" do we see today? Are they valid or not?
6. What are the dangers of seeking "signs"?
7. What is the purpose of the "unusual"?
8. Should we seek such "signs"? Why or why not?
9. How do "signs" relate to church growth?
10. What do you think would happen if a true spiritual awakening burst on the scene?

CHAPTER 12

PUTTING IT ALL TOGETHER

This book has attempted to show the intrinsic relationship between spiritual awakening and church growth. Hopefully, it has become evident that revival movements, born in the power of the Holy Spirit and the sovereign grace of God, always bring a new influx of life and vitality throughout the church. This truth relates to any congregation, regardless of location or size. When revival fires fall in a consuming manner, God's people experience new life, and many new converts come to Christ. Entire communities are sometimes transformed. The church takes on a spirit of robust health that brings warmth and attractiveness to the congregations. Unbelieving people observe this and are drawn by such warmth to God's salvation. Consequently, church growth ensues.

This emphasis on spiritual awakening is not meant to discourage a church from using biblically sound, intelligently conceived church growth programs and ministries. To the contrary, solid church growth methodologies have a definite and proper place. But undergirding such programming must be a genuine moving of the Spirit God. This is essential if these growth methods are to have a positive impact on the growth of the church and the kingdom of God.

This book may sound as though I am saying that a spiritual revival is a panacea for all the church's ills. An overemphasis on spiritual awakenings may imply that a revival movement removes all sin and solves all congregational problems. Such is not true; many mountains remain to be scaled. But it must be granted that a true move of the Holy Spirit in awakening power will do more to cure an ailing church and bring spiritual health than any humanistic effort we may undertake.

In the light of these realities, the urgency rests upon all of us who truly want our churches to grow to seek a genuine spiritual awakening that will sweep over the church and land. Therefore, let us put the proper emphasis on these principles. Let us put first things first. Let us pray sincerely, "Thy kingdom come." God grant us grace to establish and maintain proper priorities and save ourselves from "evangelical humanism."

In today's society with its deteriorating morals and ethics, the only real hope for a bright future is in a historic, biblically based awakening. This means the church has a price to pay to see God move in revival power. To use church growth methods without the foundation of spiritual realities not only puts the cart before the horse; it also fails to lay a foundation that will make church programs lasting and meaningful. We must not build upon the sand, as Jesus urged in the closing words of his Sermon on the Mount (Matt. 7:24–29). The enterprise of seeking spiritual awakening must revolve around the ministry of sacrificial prayer. The trumpet call to prayer must be loudly sounded once again. Before great growth occurs, great prayer must be made. As E. M. Bounds put it,

> There is no power like that of prevailing prayer—of Abraham pleading for Sodom, Jacob wrestling in the stillness of the night, Moses standing in the breach, Hannah intoxicated with sorrow, David heartbroken with remorse and grief, Jesus in sweat of blood. Add to this list from the records of the church your personal observation and experience, and always there is the cost of passion unto blood. Such prayer prevails. It turns ordinary mortals into people of power. It brings power. It brings fire. It brings rain. It brings life. It brings God.[1]

The field truly is ripe for harvest in many areas of our nation today—actually, in many parts of the world. May God move us to pray and grant us the thrill and joy of seeing the Holy Spirit once again revive his work and the church grow gloriously to the praise of our Lord Jesus Christ. Remember the prayer of Habakkuk? The prophet prayed:

LORD, I have heard the report about Thee and I fear.
O LORD, revive Thy work in the midst of the years,
In the midst of the years make it known;
In wrath remember mercy.
God comes from Teman,
And the Holy One from Mount Paran. [Selah.
His splendor covers the heavens,
And the earth is full of His praise.
His radiance is like the sunlight.
(Hab. 3:2–4a)

THE PROBLEMS WITH PROCESS THOUGHT

Process thought leaves one with disquieting theological and philosophical issues. Despite the popularity of the movement, these process theologians project themselves into a precarious position. First, they place themselves on shaky theological and philosophical grounds because most of them will grant that God is the Creator of all reality. But if their process presuppositions are true, then God has created an order of reality (four-dimensional time and space) to which he is subject and cannot quite cope with, at least at this stage in time. Thus, they make God, the Creator of time, subject to time.

The question then immediately rears its stubborn head: How could God possibly create something, like time, greater or "stronger" than himself? Anything God is subject to and cannot "handle" surely stands as "stronger" or greater than him. How could God, who created time and space, be subject to it? This, of course, is nonsense.

If God truly did create the entire time-space order, how could it ascend and hold sway over God? Einstein has shown us that time and space are interrelated relative aspects of reality. Human beings are in a "time-space capsule," in Einstein's words. Thus, if God created space, he created time. How could *any* creator create *any* order greater than oneself? Actually, process thought makes time the ultimate principle, not God, if God is subject to it. The time goal of process thus becomes all but God himself. That is philosophically very questionable, let alone biblical.

The Bible says, "With the Lord one day is as a thousand years, and a thousand years as one day" (2 Pet. 3:8). God transcends time, not vice versa. However, these thinkers may retort, there are certain situations God has created that by their very nature ascend above God; thus, he cannot cope with them—like the "inevitability" of evil and suffering in the light of human freedom. This line becomes a very dubious admission, for if they say God is ultimate, this precipitates a sort of ultimate dualism: God and the "inevitable situation." No serious Christian theologian or philosopher can abide such a dualism. It all but produces a quasi-philosophical polytheism.

The process thinkers state, however, that God will one day conquer all foes; therefore, it is not an *ultimate* dualism. God has not constructed something he will not be able to handle, at least some time in the future, they argue. It seems almost as if they are quoting an old proverb, "Time will heal all wounds." Their argument still leaves God on a finite time-space plane (even the secular scientists know that time and space are finite, relative, and interrelated realities), so we are still left with God creating something "greater" than himself in that he is subject to it. Thus, the "time process" is an ultimate entity, and one is left once more with a dualism or time as God.

But "time" is just *one* of our four dimensions. Further, quantum physics tell us there are seven or more additional dimensions beyond our four. Thus, process positions are simply untenable. There are better ways to solve the problem of evil and suffering. Process theology actually falls to the ground in a shambles of inner contradictions if not outright absurdities. God relates to people in their changing attitudes and actions, but God in his essence is true to himself, a constant personhood that does not change. The God of the Bible is revealed as ultimate, infinite, transcendent, sovereign, and immutable. He is infinitely beyond the bounds of creation and infinitely above the reasons of all intelligent creatures. He is Lord!

Other views that cast question marks over the sovereignty of God are not quite as serious or always pressed to the point as the views of the process theologians. So-called "liberation theology" is such a case. Although this theology does not have criticisms of the idea of an infinite God, the emphasis on certain aspects of the theology of the Most High tends to minimize his sovereignty. The same could probably be said for some forms of feminist theology as well. And in this quest, we turn to the final authority, the Holy Scripture.

Are we justified in turning to the Bible? An investigation of this issue stands in order. Turn to Appendix B for this argument.

BIBLICAL AUTHORITY AND EPISTEMOLOGY

Epistemology? What is it, and how does it emerge as the crux of the matter concerning biblical authority? Let me explain. *Epistemology* is the technical philosophical term that means the study of how a person receives and arrives at truth. It describes the basic thought system we devise for ourselves that becomes the criterion by which we judge what is real and true.

One's epistemology is vitally important. It becomes the means of discovering what we consider genuinely real and true, thus authoritative. All of us have an epistemological thought structure that we operate from.

The question is: What are the epistemological principles—or "presuppositions," as the professional philosophers call them—that form the basis of how we judge something to be true and thus reflect reality? Here are a few:

- Rationalism. If someone says, "Two plus two equals four," we rationally put that together and agree with the statement. We acknowledge it to be true and real.
- Empiricism, i.e. sense perception. If we see, touch, taste, or hear something, we normally think it to be real and true.
- Intuition. We are confronted by some concepts that we just sense, intuitively, to be true.

- A Priori concepts. A few concepts are "given," for example, self-consciousness; I know that "I am."
- Revelation. Christians have traditionally believed that God breaks in on us and reveals himself. This is how we learn things about God that we could learn no other way. Further, the supreme revelation of God came in the person of Jesus Christ, for he is the Son of God coming as a man to dwell among us. The record of this supreme unfolding of God is found in the Bible. Moreover, most Christians believe that the Bible was inspired by God in such a fashion that it is a true and trustworthy guide in these matters. Of course, epistemologists may repudiate this idea.

Most Christian thinkers, radical or conservative, have no quarrel with what has been projected so far. But now comes the crunch! No problem rears its ugly head for any of us as long as none of the above epistemological presuppositions conflict with one another. If they do, however, then we are in trouble.

Let me give an example. Some time back I was in my garage working when suddenly I heard a train passing by. I said to myself, "That train sounds very near." Then I suddenly realized I do not even live near a railroad track. Yet I was sure I heard a train. So I struggled to "put it together." The problem was with my empirical faculties. My sense perceptions had come into conflict with my rational capabilities. As I struggled to resolve the clash, it dramatically hit me: a tornado sounds like a train. I ran outside, and to my horror, a destructive tornado was bearing down only a few hundred yards away. When I saw that, my dilemma was solved. I ran as fast as I could for shelter!

Do you grasp the "epistemological situation" I was in? To put it in philosophical terms, when one of my presuppositions collided with another, I had to resolve the conflict. So I frantically searched about in my mind, trying to find a way to "put it all together." Finally I asked myself, What am I going to accept—my empiricism or my rationalization? I was forced to make a choice as to which epistemological presupposition was to have final authority as I tried to arrive at truth and reality. In this particular case, I simply could not accept my sense perception as a final authority when I "heard a train" close by.

Actually, we all go through these kinds of exercises constantly, but most of the time we do it unconsciously. We do it virtually by habit. We rarely think about it unless it comes to us dramatically as a conflict of epistomological presuppositions, as in the case above between my sense perception and my rationalism.

WHERE IT ALL LEADS

You can now probably see where we are headed as we tread through these dusty details of epistemology. There really is a goal and point to this: What if my rational, empirical faculties come into conflict with *revealed truth*—what the Bible says about Jesus Christ? For example, Jesus walking on the water. We think rationally that no one can walk on the water; yet the Scriptures tell us Jesus did. This creates a real conflict of presuppositional experiences. What is going to surface for me as the final authority in the clash of these epistemological presuppositions? Will it be my rational faculties or my revelational declarations? That is the real crunch.

For me, *revelation* is the final court of appeal in the things of God. Christians have opted for the biblical account throughout the ages. The Bible has been the traditional authoritative word for almost two thousand years.

Of course, if there is no conflict between different epistemological presuppositions, we certainly should not raise problems. If revelation agrees with what one empirically perceives or can be reasoned out rationally, so much the better. If they complement one another—as they often do—that is fine. But if a conflict arises and we must make a decision between two or more competing presuppositions, I confess that revelation is my choice.

THE FIRST LINE OF DEFENSE

The skeptic retorts that you cannot *prove* revelation. You have to exercise faith to accept revealed ideas. True! Yet there is something very important here that we all need to realize: You cannot "prove" any epistemological presupposition, be it rationalism, empiricism, or whatever. They are all *presuppositions,* not *proven facts.* It is impossible to prove empiricism empirically, rationalism rationally. You are forced to take them all "by faith." This is most important to understand. In principle, empirical and rational ideas are no more self-authenticating than revealed concepts. They all "beg the question."

For example, you must accept empirical processes to arrive at empirical data. We tend to assume that rational and empirical ideas are self-proving only because we habitually trust our sense perceptions—not to mention worshiping at the shrine of rational, empirical science. Yet a bit of reflection will quickly show us we cannot totally trust our eyes and ears. They really do deceive us at times, as do rationalism and intuition. All epistemological factors are, in principle, *moves of faith.* Philosophical epistemologists know this. This is a fundamental fact of epistemology that few competent thinkers deny. Still, what is the point?

THE POINT

First, this principle puts revelation *on an equal epistemological footing with all other presuppositions,* at least in principle. Empirical, rational ideas are no more proven "facts" than are revelational concepts. They are all presuppositions. You simply cannot rule revelation out of court because it calls for "faith." They all demand "faith." That is the first vital point.

Second, and of equal importance, in all our inevitable epistemological endeavors as we struggle to come to grips with truth and reality, we must ask ourselves: What are we after anyway? The obvious answer is a *coherent world.* We want our world to "hang together" and thus make sense. This is why I struggled mentally when I encountered the tornado. We abhor our inner world coming apart and going off in diverse directions. Those who experience that phenomenon regularly and who never resolve the conflicts are known as psychotics.

So the issue becomes this: Does putting the presupposition of revelation first (which for all practical purposes means putting the Bible first) make for a *more* coherent world than if I were to elevate some other epistemological principle as "king of the hill" in my thinking process? Is my world more real if revelation comes first? That is the ultimate question.

You have already sensed my answer. I say, definitely yes! There is solid reason for such an affirmation: We cannot discover things we need to know about God and ultimate reality by our rational and empirical mind alone, as helpful as these faculties are in experience. How can our limited finite capabilities scale the wall up to the ultimate truth? It simply cannot be done. If we are to learn of God, he must come to us in revelation.

Furthermore, God and ultimate reality are what matter most. To know him is life's highest quest. Life does not make sense without an experiential knowledge of God. Therefore, we are shut up to revelation. So we must turn to the Scriptures, since the Bible records a continuing revelation of God.

THE CONCLUSION

When we turn to revelation, we find our world far more coherent. When we put the revelation first, the world of reality "hangs together." It is the most coherent worldview. A purely empirical, rational approach, for example, may give the answer to some "how" questions, but it can never give answers to the ultimate "why" of reality. For those answers we must turn to God and his revelation. This is a central reason why a revelational epistemology makes more sense. Again, if no conflict arises between revelation and human reason, do not raise a problem. But when it does—*and it surely does at times*—revelation of God becomes the final epistemological authority. There I find Ultimate Truth that matters most in our apprehension of reality.

Furthermore, our world of reality makes far better sense—is more coherent—if we allow revelational truth in our system of thought. *Reality is far more coherent* if we make revelation (the Bible) our final authority. But all these statements imply the Bible is a revelation of God. Can the Scriptures be defended on these grounds? First, let us look deeper into a revelational epistemology.

THE FINAL DEFENSE FOR REVELATION

The previous statements on divine revelation can be defended on the basis of how we apprehend God. When God breaks in on us, how do we conceive him? He comes to us as "transcendent," "other," "beyond," "mystery," and such. Even the more radical thinkers will normally grant this. He could hardly be "God," and be otherwise.

When we say God is "transcendent," "mystery," "beyond," "other," etc., we are trying to say God is ultimate as over against finite. This is how we apprehend God if he is God at all. If we put these basic religious ideas in epistemological terms, we are forced to say that God is "suprarational," i.e. above rationalism—and "above" is to be taken seriously. God is not merely *super*rational (a better thinker than you and I) but *supra*rational (He "thinks" on a plane that we cannot attain in our finitude).

If God is like that, and surely he is, then we are forced to rely on revelation. I cannot think or cognize suprarationally. We can never build a computer complex enough to work on a *supra*rational level. If we could, the computer would be God, and we would have created him. But that is absurd. Thus, we are forced into a revelational corner as we try to think about God and form thought structures about him. God must come to us on our level. Therefore, if he does not reveal himself, we will never know what we need to know about him. How the empirical-rationalists can content themselves with their epistemological system and still try to hang on to a God who is "beyond" and "mystery" is a mystery. Yet they often put themselves in that peculiar stance.

Of course, our finite faculties can tell us something about God. "The heavens declare the glory of God" (Ps. 19:1 KJV). We are not to disparage empirical, rational truth. Still, we can never know what we need to know about a God who *redeems* without revelation. *God must speak.*

THE CONCLUSION AND FINALITY OF GOD'S REVELATION

Revelation is exactly what God did. This is the meaning of the Incarnation; the suprarational Son of God became rational so we could apprehend him. Therefore, through him we learn about God. And again, *it simply had to be this way.* Just as the great German theologian Rudolf Otto put in his well-known book *Idea of the Holy,* revelation becomes mandatory, and it was accomplished in the Incarnation of the Son of God. This is the greatest event in all creation. God came to us in Christ.

THE VITAL QUESTION ON BIBLICAL AUTHORITY

How do we learn about this incarnational revelation? This is the vital question. The answer is obvious. It is in the Bible that we learn of God's revelation. There the details of God's self-disclosure are recorded. There we learn about Jesus Christ. The Scriptures are our only source. Rationalism and empiricism will never reveal all we need to know about God. Furthermore, the biblical recording of the revelation is given by inspiration. We sense that as we read. The most radical thinkers grant some form of inspiration of the Scriptures. So we turn to the Bible as our final and only word, and it is clear what the Scriptures state concerning the person of Christ. A biblical epistemology is a faith presupposition, but so is everything else. A coherent worldview takes God at his Word.

When we state, "I turn to the Bible," we must come to it with sensible principles of interpretation. Furthermore, most Christians hold that God speaks *directly* in a revelational fashion through the Bible. As we turn to the Scriptures, we not only encounter truth about God; we encounter him. The summary of it all is simple: The Bible stands as the authoritative, revelational guide to learn about God and to be introduced to him. The Bible is the authoritative Word of God.

NOTES

Preface

1. David Beer, *50 Ways to Unleash the Potential of Your Church* (Eastbourne: Kingsway Publications, 1999), Prologue; italics added.

Chapter 1

1. Donald McGavran, *The Bridges of God* (New York: Friendship Press, 1955).

2. Donald McGavran, *Understanding Church Growth*, 2nd ed. (Grand Rapids: Eerdmans, 1980).

3. Rick Warren, *The Purpose Driven Church: Growth Without Compromising Your Message and Mission* (Grand Rapids: Zondervan, 1995).

4. See Thom S. Rainer, *The Bridger Generation* (Nashville: Broadman & Holman Publishers, 1997).

5. Ralph Neighbor Jr. and Carl Thomas, *Target-Group Evangelism* (Nashville: Broadman Press, 1975), 17.

6. Jack Burton, *England Needs Revival* (London: S.C.M. Press, Ltd., 1995), 48.

7. Donald McGavran, *Understanding Church Growth*, 196, as quoted in *The Outpouring of the Spirit in Revival and Awakening and Its Issue in Church Growth*, by J. Edwin Orr, 1984, p. 10.

8. Jonathan Goforth, *When the Spirit's Fire Swept Korea,* 1943, pp. 12 and 16 (quoted by McGavran, *Understanding Church Growth),* as quoted by J. Edwin Orr.

9. Allen D. Clark, *History of the Korean Church,* 1961, pp. 130–131; cf. all standard texts, as quoted by J. Edwin Orr.

10. McGavran, 6, 186, and passim.

CHAPTER 2

1. James M. Wall, ed., *Theologians in Transition* (New York: Crossroad Publishing Co., 1981), 77.

2. It seems so much theology is, in the final analysis, a "reaction" theology, that is, reacting against theological fads. The "death of God" theology was certainly a fad and is now quite dead itself. How important to realize a true biblical theology never passes off in a faddist fashion.

3. Norman Pittenger, *Catholic Faith in a Process Perspective* (Maryknoll, N.Y.: Orbis Books, 1981), 21–22. This brief quotation from Pittenger is not to imply that Pittenger's entire approach is found in such a few words.

4. Paul Tillich, *The Protestant Era* (Chicago: University of Chicago Press, 1983), 202.

5. Hugh Ross, *Creation and Time* (Colorado Springs: Navpress, 1994), 154.

6. G. Wayne Dorsett, *Developing a New Members Class for Perimeter Road Baptist Church, Valdosta, Georgia* (unpublished Doctor of Ministry Project, Samford University, 1998), 62–64.

CHAPTER 3

1. Elisabeth O'Connor, *Eighth Day of Creation* (Waco: Word Books, 1971), 13.

2. John R. W. Stott, *One People* (London: Falcon Books, 1969), 24.

3. Judson W. Van DeVenter and Winfield S. Weeder, "I Surrender All."

4. Source unknown.

CHAPTER 4

1. Stephen Olford, *The Way of Holiness* (Wheaton, Ill.: Crossway Books, 1998), 137–38. Permission granted.

2. J. H. Fairchild, "Introduction" to Charles G. Finney's *Systematic Theology* (abridged) (Minneapolis: Bethany Fellowship, Inc., 1976), as quoted in *Charles Grandison Finney and the Birth of Modern Evangelism* by Lewis A. Drummond.

3. Ibid.

4. Charles G. Finney, *Memoirs of Charles G. Finney* (New York: Fleming H. Revell Company, 1876), 18–23.

CHAPTER 5

1. Ernest F. Stoeffler, *Continental Pietism and Early American Christianity* (Grand Rapids: William B. Eerdmans Publishing Company, 1976), 9.

2. Ernest F. Stoeffler, *The Rise of Evangelical Pietism* (Leiden, Netherlands: E. J. Brill, 1971), 29.

3. Ibid., 115.

4. Ibid., 9.

5. Donald Bloesch, *The Evangelical Renaissance* (Grand Rapids, Mich.: Wm. B. Eerdmans Publishing Co., 1973), 106.

6. Ibid.

7. Ibid.

8. Ibid., 108.

9. Ibid.

10. Ibid., 109.

11. Stoeffler, *The Rise of Evangelical Pietism*, 131.

12. Bloesch, 110.

13. Stoeffler, *The Rise of Evangelical Pietism*, 20.

14. G. Campbell Morgan, *The Gospel According to Matthew* (New York: Flemeng H. Revell Co., 1934), 219–20.

15. R. A. Torrey, *The Power of Prayer* (Grand Rapids: Zondervan Publishing House, 1955), 74.

16. Ibid., 135.

17. Ibid., 137.

18. Leonard Ravenhill, *A Treasury of Prayer* (Minneapolis: Bethany Fellowship, Inc., 1961), 52.

19. Rick Warren, *The Purpose Driven Church* (Grand Rapids: Zondervan Publishing House, 1995), 138–51.

CHAPTER 6

1. This does not imply the erroneous doctrine of universalism.

2. Oswald J. Smith, *The Cry of the World* (London, Marshall, Morgan and Scott, 1959), 46.

3. From Walter B. Knight, *Three Thousand Illustrations for Christian Service* (Grand Rapids: Wm. B. Eerdmans Publishing Co., 1952).

4. Douglas Webster, *Yes to Mission* (London: S.C.M. Press Ltd., 1966), 20.

5. C. H. Dodd, *The Apostolic Preaching and Its Development* (London: Hodder and Stoughton, 1936), 7.

6. Ibid., 8.

7. Ibid.

8. Ibid., 24.

9. Ibid., 17.

10. Ibid., 25.

11. Ibid., 61.

12. John R. W. Stott, *The Message of Acts* (Downers Grove, Ill., InterVarsity Press, 1990), 312.

13. Ibid., 280–81.

CHAPTER 7

1. W. A. Criswell, *These Issues We Must Face* (Grand Rapids: Zondervan Publishers, 1953), 33–34.

2. George Barna, *Evangelism That Works* (Ventura, Calif.: Regal Books, 1995), 15.

3. Ibid., 132.

CHAPTER 8

1. James Burns, *Revivals: Their Laws and Leaders* (Grand Rapids: Baker Book House, 1960), 138–39.

2. Dewey M. Beegle, *Scripture, Tradition, and Infallibility* (Grand Rapids: Wm. B. Eerdmans Publishing Co., 1973).

3. Billy Graham, *The Holy Spirit* (Waco, Tex.: Word Books, 1978), 43.

4. Ibid., 66–67.

5. Andrew Murray, *The Holiest of All* (Springdale, Penn.: Whitaker House, 1996), 50.

6. Keith Wiginton on a plaque.

7. Murray, *The Holiest of All,* 49.

CHAPTER 9

1. Eric W. Hayden, *Spurgeon on Revival* (Grand Rapids: Zondervan Publishing House, 1962), 13.

2. Ibid., 14.

3. Ibid.

4. Charles H. Spurgeon, *Autobiography*, vol. 2 (London: Pasomore and Alabaster, 1899), 221.

5. Stephen F. Olford, *Lord, Open the Heavens* (Wheaton, Ill.: Harold Shaw Publishers, 1962), 60.

6. Nathaniel Emmons, *A System of Divinity* (Boston: Crocker and Brewster, 1842), 2:327.

7. William Carey, *An Inquiry into the Obligations of Christians to Use Means for the Conversion of the Heathen, 1792* (London: Baptist Missionary Society, 1934), 77.

8. Timothy Dwight, *Sermons* (New Haven: Hezekiah, Howe, Durrie, and Peck, 1828), 1:242.

9. Lewis A. Drummond, *Eight Keys to Biblical Revival* (Minneapolis: Bethany House Publishers, 1994), 115.

10. Evelyn Christenson, *What Happens When Women Pray* (Wheaton, Ill.: Victor Books, 1975), 113.

11. Helen S. Shoemaker, *Prayer and Evangelism* (Waco, Tex.: Word Books, 1974), 58.

CHAPTER 10

1. Thom S. Rainer, *Giant Awakenings* (Nashville: Broadman & Holman Publishers, 1995), 151.

CHAPTER 11

1. Mendell Taylor, *Exploring Evangelism* (Kansas City: Beacon Hill Press, 1964), 409.
2. Ibid., 410.
3. Ibid.
4. Ibid., 412.
5. Bertha Smith, *Go Home and Tell* (Nashville: Broadman & Holman Publishers, 1996), 51–52.
6. From Allan Hermert and Perry Miller, eds., *The Great Awakening* (Indianapolis: Bobbs-Merrill Educational Publications, 1967), 518–19.

CHAPTER 12

1. Source unknown.